LIGHTNING KID

64 Winning Lessons from the Boy Who Became Five-Time World Chess Champion

AF675263

Viswanathan Anand, known fondly as Vishy, is one of the most prominent names in chess. Over the three decades since he turned Grandmaster, he has won five World Championship titles among innumerable other tournaments and has continued to push past barriers to remain among the world's top chess players. His achievements have helped inspire a generation of chess players in India. Vishy is an astronomy buff, and an avid reader of maths, economics and current affairs. He loves to travel, and particularly enjoys wildlife safaris. He supports the cause of Indian sports, as Director of Olympic Gold Quest and mentor at the Westbridge Anand Chess Academy. Anand is the Ambassador for the World Wildlife Fund (WWF) India's Environment Education programme and a spokesperson for the NIIT Foundation to create awareness about cybersecurity.

Susan Ninan is a sports writer with ESPN and is based in Bengaluru. She has previously worked with the *Times of India,* and has covered major sporting events like the Commonwealth Games and the World Chess Championships. When she is not writing on sport or travelling to find a story, she loves sniffing around bookstores and going backpacking, or at best making plans for the latter.

LIGHTNING KID

64 Winning Lessons from the Boy Who Became Five-Time World Chess Champion

VISWANATHAN ANAND

with

SUSAN NINAN

Adapted for young readers by

Vatsala Kaul Banerjee

hachette
INDIA

First published in paperback in 2026 by Hachette India
(Registered name: Hachette Book Publishing India Pvt. Ltd)
An Hachette UK company
www.hachetteindia.com

1

Text Copyright © 2026 Viswanathan Anand

This edition has been adapted for young readers from
Mind Master: Winning Lessons from a Champion's Life, published by
Hachette India in hardback in 2019 and in paperback in 2022.

Viswanathan Anand asserts the moral right to be identified as the author of this work.

Illustrations of chess pieces and full page illustration on page viii
by Mohit Suneja; vector illustrations of chess pieces from Vecteezy.com/SAM KAL;
diagrams in the preliminary pages by Syed Salahuddin.

Photographs copyright information: **page 82:** courtesy of *New In Chess*;
page 113: © Eric van Reem, courtesy of Eric van Reem; **page 119:** © Amruta Mokal/
ChessBase India, courtesy of Amruta Mokal/ChessBase India;
page 168: Wikimedia Commons: Government Open Data License - India (GODL),
http://pib.nic.in/newsite/photo.aspx?photoid=18016;
page 239: © David Llada, courtesy of David Llada.
The remaining images are from the private archives of Viswanathan Anand.

All rights reserved. No part of the publication may be reproduced, stored in a retrieval system (including but not limited to computers, disks, external drives, electronic or digital devices, e-readers, websites), or transmitted in any form or by any means (including but not limited to cyclostyling, photocopying, docutech or other reprographic reproductions, mechanical, recording, electronic, digital versions) without the prior written permission of the publisher, nor be otherwise circulated in any form of binding or cover other than that in which it is published and without a similar condition being imposed on the subsequent purchaser.

The views and opinions provided in this book are the author's own and the facts are as reported by him and have been verified to the extent possible. The publishers are not in any way liable for the same.

Old names of some places, such as Madras and others, have been used only to maintain the historicity and genuineness of the information or the reference used.

Subsequent edition/reprint specifications may be subject to change including but not limited to cover or inside finishes, paper, text colour and/or colour sections.

ISBN 978-93-5731-790-0

Hachette Book Publishing India Pvt. Ltd
4th & 5th Floors, Corporate Centre
Plot No. 94, Sector 44, Gurugram – 122003, India

Typeset by Manmohan Kumar, Delhi

Printed and bound in India
by Manipal Technologies Limited

FSC
www.fsc.org
MIX
Paper | Supporting
responsible forestry
FSC™ C043100

For my mother, who told me to always write down my thoughts, good or bad. She said, 'One day you will read them and realize how beautiful they are.'

* * *

Know Chess More through International Master V. Anand

Chess is a game which originated in India and spread to Persia and from there spread to the world. Its rules are very simple and is a battle of 2 Armies of 16 Pieces, over a Board of 64 squares. It is in reality infinitely complex.

The number of possible moves in a chess game is staggering. In fact, no one has ever been able to determine just how many there are. One investigator calculated a number on the order of 10^{120} — that is, the figure one followed by 120 zeros. The choices for the first 15 moves alone number more than 300 thousand million.

The world Chess Federation gives two titles to Players of extra-ordinary achievements. One is International Master Title and the other is Grand

V. Anand

19

ME IN THE SCHOOL MAGAZINE AROUND 1986–87

'Regrets, I've had a few
But then again, too few to mention
I did what I had to do
And saw it through without exemption.
I planned each charted course
Each careful step along the byway...
Yes, there were times, I'm sure you knew
When I bit off more than I could chew
But through it all, when there was doubt
I ate it up and spit it out
I faced it all and I stood tall
And did it my way...'

'*My Way*', Lyrics by Paul Anka
Sung by Frank Sinatra in 1969

CONTENTS

JOIN ME IN A GAME!
Top Tips from Milestone Matches

PIECE BY PIECE
The Power of Every Move

THE OPENING

When I was young, I didn't know that my life was going to be such an adventure.

I didn't imagine that it would have kings and queens, knights and bishops, and even the pawns would turn out to be powerful characters in a quest played out on stark black and white squares – again, and again, and once more. That I was going to be the protagonist who would ride to different parts of the world to brave challenging contests, the one who would decide the direction this mission would take, the speed at which it would be completed and whether I would succeed – or end up disappointed.

That sounds like a fantasy. It became my reality.

Chess is all that to me, and more. It grew from something I was good at to an overriding passion, and then to a career that has filled my entire life. It was, of course, very different from a regular nine-to-five job. It required me to show up in one or the other country, my chess know-how somehow miraculously packed into my head, my brain sharpened like a pointy pencil, my body trained for hours of stillness, my game wits all about me…to be able to compete with my opponents, who were more often than not the best players of chess in the whole wide world. Those tough matches opened the door to the biggest stage of all – the World Chess Championship. I won it in 2000, and then again in 2007, 2008, 2010 and 2012, holding the undisputed title from 2007 to 2013.

I was known for my rapid playing speed when I was quite young – around 10–11 years old – and that's why the media nicknamed me 'Lightning Kid'. I must admit that, like most kids, I was impatient and wanted to get through my competition as quickly as possible, but

A SPEEDY GONZALES. . .OF CHESS

I had, of course, no awareness of my own 'lightning-ness'. It was just how it was.

Rapid and blitz chess weren't a thing then – FIDE, the governing body of international chess competitions, started a championship for those only in 2012, the year I won the World Chess Championship the fifth time around. Speed, of course, is not the only thing that has changed in chess over the years. If one compares today's chess to the earliest formal tournaments, then one could say a few rules have changed, such as those for draws, stalemates and the movement of pawns. But the biggest difference has been the entry of computers.

First, the intervention of computers has affected 'not knowing'. Earlier, when the most accomplished chess players competed, it was a mystery – and a marvel! – to see what move they would conjure up out of their thinking hat. These days, the games may be streamed live on the internet, and you, as the spectator, can run a chess engine on the computer, and it reveals the best moves. An evaluation of these moves can instantly tell us if the player has made an error.

Sometimes commentators look at these moves to know what would have been the best move for that player and base their comments on that. Many commentators, however, still rely only on 'human' inputs – those that the players are making. But the spectators are already on the chess engine…and the word on the 'mistake' is soon out there on social media and likely going viral.

Second, cheating has crept into the game. For instance, in two infamous cases, a player allegedly got help from a computer during his frequent toilet breaks, and another reportedly hid a computer device in his shoe! Because of such incidents, players are now made to go through metal detectors in some tournaments.

Most importantly, the surge of computers in the game plan has transformed how players prepare for tournaments, and especially their openings. There are zillions of opening options in chess databases, to which more are added daily, and players can prep by testing any number of openings in a chess engine. And this process can show unique, new and potentially successful moves that no one before has ever thought of!

That's a lot of new changes to make way for.

And that's not all. Chess has become more of a spectator sport than it ever was. Millions of people around the world watch chess tournaments. And more often than not, they are watching young Indians play. Chennai, where I come from, has long been established as the chess capital of India, and many, many youngsters – several of whom I mentor as part of my work with my WestBridge Anand Chess Academy (WACA) – are winning accolades and titles.

Yes, the chess universe is shifting, but think about this – the game itself has stayed more or less the same for around 600 years. The board, the pieces, the way they are moved – it's still the same. Any chess game is still that tight, high-suspense contest it always was, where each move can make or break you.

That's why my story, I feel, will make sense to you. This is not an autobiography but the highlights – and many 'low lights' too – of my life that I have picked out especially to share with you.

Here are a few questions I have thought about over the years, and if you too have wondered about them or had them at the back of your mind, then we're on!

- Is winning about picking out an option from a vast database of good moves, or is it something more?
- Does failure teach us something besides telling us that the other person did better that one time?
- How long should one give oneself to decide if one is good, or *really* good, or even *great* at anything?
- Can success in a game – or in life – be the happy result of instinct, or improvisation, or does it always need a calculated and planned route?
- And why does a person like me, who has stored many thousand chess moves in his head, often forget where his keys are? (Haha. Let me know if you know.)

This book is about all those things – a bit about me, a lot about chess, and a whole lot about that vast and exciting common space where chess and I become one.

In the pages that follow, I have shared my roller-coaster adventure with you, my ups and downs – and so much in between – as stories rather than as instruction. I'll be thrilled if you find in them something that helps you, makes you think or is useful in your life.

Because yesterday's game becomes today's lesson.

And today's learner becomes tomorrow's champion.

Join me in the game!

Love,
Vishy

YES, I WAS JUST LIKE YOU!

READY, SET...CHESS!

The Basics of the Game

The chessboard has 64 squares: 8 rows, also called 'ranks' (numbers 1–8) and 8 columns, also called 'files' (letters a–h). Each square has a name, like e4 or c6. That's how players record their moves.

8	a8	b8	c8	d8	e8	f8	g8	h8
7	a7	b7	c7	d7	e7	f7	g7	h7
6	a6	b6	c6	d6	e6	f6	g6	h6
5	a5	b5	c5	d5	e5	f5	g5	h5
4	a4	b4	c4	d4	e4	f4	g4	h4
3	a3	b3	c3	d3	e3	f3	g3	h3
2	a2	b2	c2	d2	e2	f2	g2	h2
1	a1	b1	c1	d1	e1	f1	g1	h1
	a	b	c	d	e	f	g	h

THE PIECES AND HOW THEY MOVE

Each player has 16 pieces, either black or white: 1 king, 1 queen, 2 knights, 2 bishops, 2 rooks and 8 pawns.

King (K): Value = theoretically infinite, as losing it ends the game.

Moves in any direction (sideways, forward, back, diagonally) but only one square.

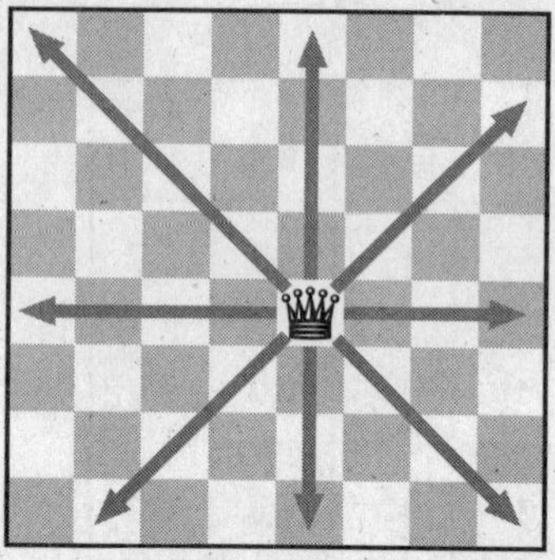

Queen (Q): Value = 9 points

Moves any number of squares in a straight line (sideways, forward, back, diagonally).

Rook (R): Value = 5 points

Moves any number of squares forward, back or sideways but not diagonally.

Bishop (B): Value = 3 points

Moves any number of squares forward or backward, but only diagonally. Always stays on the same colour squares.

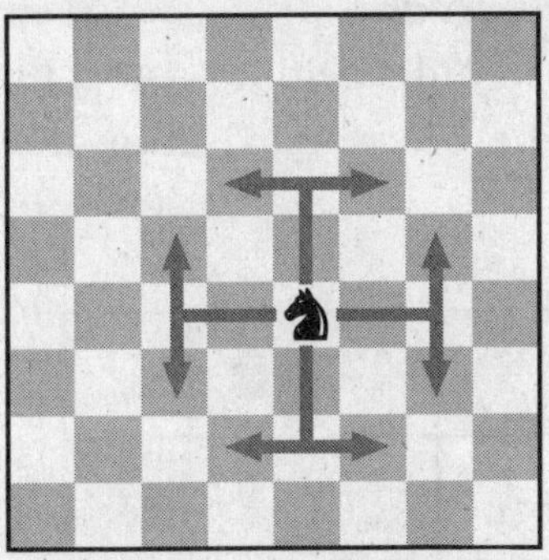

Knight (N): Value = 3 points

Moves in a capital L shape. Two squares forward/ backward and one sideways OR one square forward/ backward and two sideways. Can jump over all other pieces but may not capture them.

Pawn (No letter assigned): Value = 1 point

Only moves in the forward direction.
Pa: 1st move: goes 1 or 2 squares.
Pb: After 1st move, goes 1 square.
Pc: Capture: Diagonally 1 square only.
Pawn Promotion: Pawn reaching the other end of the board can become a queen, rook, bishop or knight.

UNDERSTANDING MOVES

White always moves first, then players take turns. The goal is to checkmate the other king – put it in danger so it cannot escape. Moves are written using the letter for the column and the number of the square. For example:

- **1. e4** → White's pawn moves to e4.
- **1... c5** → Black's pawn moves to c5.
- **2. Nf3** → White's knight jumps to f3.
- **2... d6** → Black's pawn moves to d6.

And that's how a real chess game begins – step by step, move by move! Here's the chessboard after the first two moves:

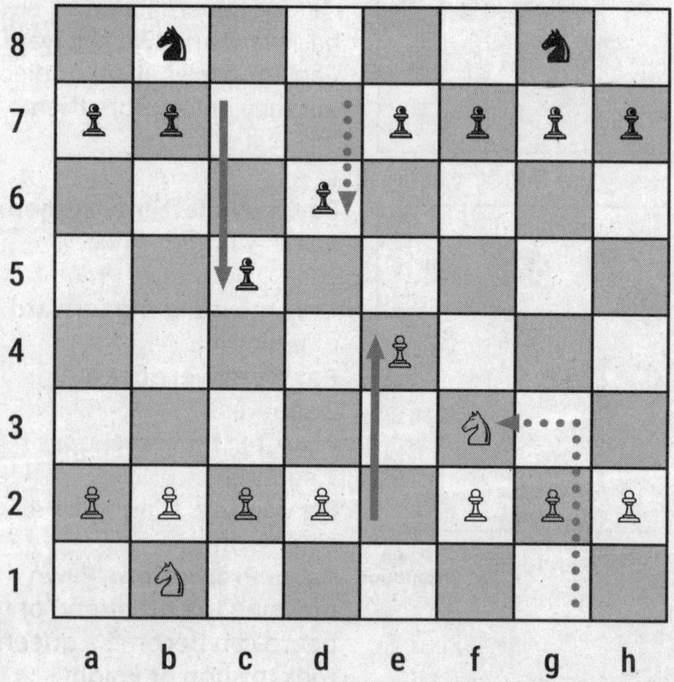

What about a capture? That is indicated by the letter 'x'. For instance:

- **Nxf6:** A knight takes a piece on f6.
- **exd5:** The pawn from the e-file moves diagonally and captures a piece on d5.

You will find several moves mentioned in the book in this way – look up this board and you will know what happened in the game!

Titles

For those who may not know, a chess **Grandmaster (GM)** is a player awarded the highest title in chess by FIDE (World Chess Federation or the International Chess Federation, known by the acronym of its French name: *Fédération Internationale des Échecs*), except for the World Champion title, which is a separate championship. To earn the GM title, a player must achieve a FIDE rating of at least 2500 and earn three Grandmaster norms in specific FIDE-sanctioned tournaments that meet rigorous criteria for tournament length, opponent requirements (including other titled players) and performance rating.

An **International Master (IM)** is a highly skilled chess player, the second-highest title awarded by FIDE, below Grandmaster. To earn the IM title, a player must achieve a FIDE rating of 2400 or higher and obtain three title norms, which are strong performances in specific international tournaments. These norms require a high-level performance rating (typically 2450+) and must be earned against a mix of titled and non-titled players from different national federations.

1

A SMALL START

Let me tell you something you don't know about me – a secret. When I was young, I loathed tennis lessons. I didn't mind the sport itself, but I was barely seven then, and the sessions started at 5:30 in the morning – hey, even the sun wasn't fully awake by then!

I was part of the junior programme at the tennis academy run by the noted coach Robin Manfred in Egmore, Madras (now Chennai), less than 5 kilometres away from the Railway bungalows on Sterling Road, where we lived.

The morning began with endless rounds of jogging around the court, meant to serve as warm-ups for the lessons to follow, but I rarely got a chance to hit the ball. We were bunched into groups and got to play just four forehands and four backhands each before it was pack-up time. The next group would troop on to the court right after.

It didn't seem worth it to me to wake up so early, and I often wondered why my parents were spending good money to have me run around a court. It was disappointing after the dreamy fantasies I had of myself chipping, charging and volleying like my hero, John McEnroe. I idolized the American tennis star, whose bright red sweatband encircled a mop of springy curls, and who threw tantrums with as much style as he did volleys and shots with the racquet, though my own nature was completely the opposite – quiet and laid-back. I didn't have his 'swagger' nor his fast 'n' furious personality.

Luckily, I had chess.

And I had my teacher, coach and loudest cheerleader all rolled into one – my mother.

Amma belonged to a family of lawyers who played chess at home, and she picked up the sport early. She had introduced chess to my brother, older than me by thirteen years, and my sister, eleven years my senior – and like the youngest child in every family, I was keen to do whatever my older siblings did – and do it better! I moved my first piece on the chessboard when I was six.

AMMA WAS MY FIRST CHESS TEACHER, AND A FRIEND AND ALLY FOR LIFE

My mother was as good at the game as one could get playing at home without formal training but was soon losing to me at the board. My sister was studying at Stella Maris College at the time. One day, on her way back home, she happened to spot a signboard that read 'Chess Club' outside a building and told us excitedly about it. A quick investigation followed, and the place turned out to be the Mikhail Tal Chess Club, named after the former Soviet great and housed at the Soviet Cultural Centre in Alwarpet.

Chess was not a sport in the limelight then, and India didn't have a Grandmaster (GM) yet. Manuel Aaron, who was the only International Master (IM) in the country when I started out, was one of the founding members of the Tal Chess Club. He was a dedicated champion of the game and had learnt Russian to be able to read (and translate) chess books into English because publications from abroad were very expensive then. The Soviet consulates in India at the time had many collaborations with Indians excelling in sports and culture, and there was also an Indo-Soviet Cultural Exchange Programme.

There was a bigger drama going on in the world at the time – between the USA and Russia, each fighting to be a superpower to foster its ideas and increase its influence on the rest of the world. You may have heard the term 'Cold War', and that's what it was because there was no direct war between them. The fact that the Soviets were establishing such clubs was part of their effort to be 'leaders' in the world – and as a spinoff of it, the Tal Club got free chess sets, chess clocks, books and magazines.

The year the Tal Chess Club was set up – 1972 – was also when the city of Reykjavik, on the coast of Iceland, played host to a match between two iconic chess greats – Bobby Fischer, who was American, and Boris Spassky, a Russian. You can imagine how that game became a symbolic tussle between the two wannabe superpowers! (I only learnt this later, of course, because I was only three at the time the match took place and was followed closely by the whole world. But it's a cool fact to share with you.)

***

Anyhow, it wasn't long before I became a regular visitor to the Tal Club. I was gawky and restless, and spent the first couple of days there watching older people play. I was very shy and wasn't sure if I should just sit at a table and start a game or wait for someone to tell me to.

Soon, a friendly gentleman there called Keshavan, who looked after the everyday work of the club, nudged me to join in the games. Amma requested him to have my name included in all the weekend tournaments hosted by the club. Three days after joining the club, I played my first tournament.

Was that a good idea? Probably not, considering I had not played chess outside of my home, but at that time it seemed the natural next step – and way more fun than merely watching others!

I lost my first three games quite quickly. I waited nervously for the fourth opponent as the clock ticked –

and he didn't turn up at all. So, I ended up with my first win in chess. Yes, it was by default, but at that time, a win was a win, and I felt its thrill.

That must have given me the push to go forward and get better at the game, for which I had to know more. There was no internet then. The world was not as closely connected as it is now, with things coming across quickly from other countries. Back then, chess books were hard to find, especially the best ones from other countries. And without strong tournaments or world-class opponents, it was tough for Indian players to improve. At that time, if you wanted information on chess, books were the only way. And where would you get them from? Hmm…you would have to wait for a kind 'uncle' or 'aunty' who lived abroad or visited foreign countries, to get you a book you wanted.

My sister, who always looked out for me, once picked up a copy of *Chess Openings: Theory and Practice* by Israel Albert Horowitz (an American IM) for me from a local bookstore. I literally chewed my way through the book – laugh if you like! – from cover to cover and digested every word faithfully. Horowitz was famous for his chess books (he wrote at least 20 of them), and for me, everything that book said was the last and final truth – to be trusted, followed and never questioned.

For many years after that, the collection of openings I depended on all the time was drawn only from the book! Later, in Manila, I got hold of Cuban world champion (the third in history) José Raúl Capablanca's *Chess Fundamentals,* American chess master Fred

Reinfeld's *How to Win Chess Games Quickly* and other books from which I learnt how to avoid getting trapped and scammed on opening.

Manila was a kind of milestone. When I was a little over eight, my father, who worked with the Indian Railways, was asked to go on a special job to Manila, the capital of the Philippines, for a year and a half. Both my brother and my sister was pursuing higher studies, so who was left to go along with the parents?

Yes, yours truly!

The Philippines is well known for its dugongs, peacock-pheasants and cassava cake, but at that time it was famous for something else as well, something that was completely up my alley…

VISHY SAYS

ONCE YOU FIGURE OUT SOMETHING YOU WANT TO DO OR GET BETTER AT, HOW TO DO IT IS ON YOU. PEOPLE CAN HELP YOU, NUDGE YOU, GUIDE YOU AND INSTRUCT YOU, BUT FINALLY, IT'S YOU WHO MUST SEEK, FIND AND ABSORB THE KNOWLEDGE NEEDED TO GO FORWARD. LEARNING IS *YOUR* JOB.

2

VANILLA (PLUS YUMMIES) IN MANILA

The most thrilling part before I actually got there was the plane ride to the Philippines, which – as most of you might know – is a country made of more than 7,000 islands in the Pacific Ocean.

We landed in Manila in November 1978, a month after an epic World Championship match was played between fellow Russians Anatoly Karpov and Viktor Korchnoi in Baguio City. The clash itself was a bitterly contested one, and weird too – as I found out later. Korchnoi had hired American yoga experts to up his game, while Karpov had a hypnotherapist; a yoghurt sent to Karpov was said to be a code, and whatnot!

My interest in chess was quite clear to everyone now, and it led my parents to take me to the venue where the match had been played. Though the hillside city was as pretty as a postcard, for a boy of my age, the match hall, which now only had empty chairs, was not exciting at all. Even the thought of a World Champion having sat there, playing a blistering game, defeating his equally strong and fiery opponent, and dashing off with the champion's trophy, failed to excite me at the time. Once I'd seen the chairs, I only wanted to get back to my comics.

That didn't mean that I was any less into chess than I was in Madras. The amazing thing that was happening in the Philippines was that a chess boom was going on, and I was lucky to be bang in the middle of it. The country was home to Asia's first GM, Eugenio Torre, and my mother was determined to do whatever she could to encourage my ability and interest in chess.

In her typical way, she persisted in finding ways for my game to improve. One of them was to find the best people to help me – and I mean THE BEST: the Grandmaster himself! She picked up the fat telephone directory (or phonebook, as it was called there) and began to look up every single 'Torre' in the country until her search was narrowed down to the most likely Torre. She circled this one.

Would you believe that when she called that number, it turned out that while she'd found the right Torre family, she had got hold of the wrong brother! Fortunately, this sibling of Eugenio Torre was a chess coach and was kind enough to suggest a good chess club for me to go to. Though I ended up not attending chess lessons in Manila, I participated regularly in the weekend tournaments at a nearby club.

Our main mode of commuting in Manila were the brightly painted Jeepneys. They were United States Army jeeps, earlier used for transporting soldiers, that had been abandoned by the troops after World War II, a long-drawn-out conflict that involved many countries. The Jeepneys, with their own iconic art and look, carry 20–25 passengers each. My mother and I would take them to and from the club, and a good game meant that I would be treated to a bucket of ice cream with tiny chunks of jelly and nuts in it at the parlour right next to our house. For sure, that was what I looked forward to the most after a win!

***

In the beginning, a trainer was hired to help me with my game. He ran me through bishop endings – these happen when each side in a chess game has a single bishop on opposite-coloured squares, and no other pieces except pawns and kings. These endings are known for being difficult to win and often result in a draw. However, some factors can make one bishop stronger than the other, which can lead to a win. It soon became clear that I already knew much of what he was trying to teach me, and the sessions were called off.

The unusual thing that happened was that while I was away at school, during the afternoons, my mother would watch an hour-long chess show on television called *Chess Today*, which analysed the games of leading players. At the end of each episode, the show's presenter would leave the viewers with a chess position to solve, answers to which had to be sent via post. The winners were mailed a chess book as a prize.

My mother – so dedicated was she to my cause – would carefully note down every position explained

HAPPY ME AFTER WINNING THE 'CHESS TODAY' PUZZLE IN MANILA IN 1979

during the show, often even painstakingly writing down all the moves for me to look at and study later. After I was home from school, Amma and I would work on the puzzle together, solve it and post the answer. I began winning so often that the organizers of the show were at their wits' end. They asked me to visit their library and help myself to as many books as I wanted, on the condition that I wouldn't send in any more answers!

It was not just chess that my mother gave me company in. She learnt swimming too, so that she could be with me in the pool at our home in Manila and became something of a lifeguard as I splashed around. She loved me no end and always wanted me to be happy! Once, when I told her about the surprised looks my classmates exchanged upon seeing her pick me up from school in a saree, she bought herself Western clothes so she could wear them when she went about with me in the Philippines.

The year and a half passed quickly, and we prepared to go back home to Madras. But that was not the last time I was in the Philippines. I was going to circle back to this country, and to that very championship hall I had visited, and the importance of that venue was going to hit me smack in my pleased-as-punch face. Because, coincidentally, that's where I would win my World Junior Championship title, nine years later.

Yet a lot was to happen…before that happened.

OPPORTUNITIES MAY BE SMALL OR BIG – MAKE USE OF EVERY ONE OF THEM TO GET AHEAD ON YOUR PATH. BUT ALSO BE SURE OF WHAT YOU KNOW, AND KNOW IT WELL, SO THAT YOU DON'T HAVE TO SPEND TIME REDOING YOUR EFFORTS.

VISHY SAYS

3

BACK IN CHENNAI

We returned to Madras in 1980 when I was ten. And, guess what, I rejoined my tennis classes. Sportspersons always have to start the day early, and it was no different for me. I woke up at 5 in the morning, reached the tennis academy in half an hour, trained there, returned home, showered, changed, rushed to school and, after classes were done, headed over to the Tal Club for chess. My days were packed. Pretty soon it was clear to everybody that my tennis was going nowhere, but my chess was, so I dropped out of tennis and focused on chess. That got me an extra blissful hour of sleep in the morning!

Besides being back home in India, that year was special because I had my first interaction with a GM, Vladimir Bagirov. At that time, there was no Indian GM. There were a few strong players, such as Manuel Aaron, who became India's first IM in 1961. He dominated Indian chess in the 1960s and 70s. Other IMs such as V. Ravikumar, T.N. Parameswaran, Raja Ravisekhar and Pravin Thipsay were important figures on the national chess scene, though they didn't break through to GM level.

You must know about chess having deep roots in Indian culture. It's amazing that chess began in India centuries ago, probably during the Gupta Empire. Back then it was called *chaturanga,* and it was all about armies – with elephants and chariots instead of rooks and bishops! The game spread to Persia and Europe through the Arabs, and eventually evolved, with changes big and small, into the game we know today.

A historical game it may well have been, but chess as a modern sport didn't have much help from official bodies in India at this time in the early 1980s. It was seen more as a 'brainy' hobby or passion, rather than a professional or mainstream sport. It was expensive and complicated to travel and stay abroad, and very few Indian players participated in international events due to these reasons. They did not get exposed to strong world-class competition or chess literature, which could deepen their understanding of the game.

The All India Chess Federation existed, but it was neither very active nor did it have influence globally. Most tournaments were local or national-level events of modest importance. In the absence of infrastructure for the sport, very few international tournaments were held in India. There were hardly any training opportunities for young chess enthusiasts and few coaches who could prepare them for world events. It was hard to find sponsors. Chess remained an amateur-level pursuit, often nurtured through local clubs, like the one I frequented.

It was here that the GM was visiting.

Vladimir Bagirov was a well-known Latvian Soviet player who had even coached the great Mikhail Tal – the man our club was named after!

He played an exhibition game simultaneously against a roomful of schoolchildren. I was quite confident of my skills, perhaps overconfident, as I could be sometimes. At one stage of the game, I offered him a draw. He looked at me, then at my board, picked up his rook and my bishop in one fell swoop and, in a thick Russian accent, asked me why I had made him the offer.

It was my first lesson in piece evaluation, and a good one. His rejection of my offer made me realize that you don't always get a draw when you offer one.

***

I was by then really good at the usual five-minute blitz games that were played at the club. It worked like this by the rules: winners could keep their place at the table, while the ones who lost had to get back in the queue and wait for another turn.

As it turned out often, I would be sitting tight at one end of the table and my opponents at the other end would change with every game. Amid the competition I had there, I was getting quite good at the game. I got to play as much as I wanted too. The contests were rarely organized by age group then, and you had to match up to players of all ages and stages, strengths and skills. So many matches being played also meant that I could observe and hold my own against all kinds of fresh theories, moves and styles of play. It was a kind of crash course that helped me grow as a player quickly over a relatively short period of time.

This suited me just fine as I was eager to learn and learnt quickly. At the club, however, I was looked upon as the cocky boy who would beat the older players at blitz games and interrupt Manuel Aaron's lectures on the tactics of Soviet GMs with unasked-for suggestions for alternative moves. A fellow player once complained to my mother that I was badly behaved. It came as a surprise to me since I wasn't that sort of person, nor did I mean to be rude or disrespectful. I was just keen to get on to the next game. I had absorbed as much as there was to know in the place at the time, and I wanted to move forward. I did this by participating in a rather crazy number of local tournaments in 1981.

That year also marked the last time I played chess with my mother. We had gone to Shimla on a family holiday and one evening, a terrible hailstorm forced us to stay in our hotel room. With nothing else to do, we played Monopoly, my favourite board game then next to chess, but soon my mother and I were launching our bishops and knights at each other. I remember that I came up with a highly ridiculous opening scheme and, even though I was a much stronger player than her, I lost. Somehow, we never sat across a board to play each other after that. Yet, we did continue to discuss chess, and she travelled with me for tournaments.

A big one was about to come up for me.

VISHY SAYS

OFTEN, IT CAN BE UP TO YOU TO FIGURE OUT THAT YOU HAVE LEARNT EVERYTHING A PERSON OR A PLACE HAS TO TEACH YOU. AT THAT JUNCTURE, PRESS TO MOVE AHEAD, TAKE A STEP FORWARD, AND MAKE SURE EVERYONE CAN SEE THAT YOU NEED BIGGER CHALLENGES. IF YOU ARE STUCK, YOU CAN DISCUSS IT WITH YOUR PARENTS, TEACHER/ COACH OR ANY MENTOR.

4

FINDING YOUR TALENT

Everyone has a special talent in one field or the other. The only difference is that some of us discover it early, while others notice it later. Either way, it's there! I believe that almost anything becomes easier the more you work at it. When you first try something new, it can feel strange or even hard. But give it five days of practice, and you will already see progress. After two weeks, you will notice that your brain has adjusted, and you are doing it much faster. It feels amazing when you realize that something you once found tricky is suddenly easy! That's the magic of practice – little by little, your effort turns into skill, and you start to enjoy what you're doing even more.

So how do you find what you're talented in? Usually, it comes from being exposed to different activities – sports, music, art, games, reading… Parents, teachers and elders often give us these 'gifts' by introducing us to new things we might not have tried ourselves. Sometimes you might discover a new interest just by trying something a friend enjoys, watching a video or joining a school club you haven't tried before.

Some people have a natural leaning towards something – so for them, learning feels smoother. A person with a talent for music, for example, may pick up rhythm quickly. An athlete may naturally have strong reflexes. But even then, talent is only the starting point. Without hard work and practice, no one goes very far.

TALENT SHOWS THE WAY, BUT PRACTICE IS WHAT CARRIES YOU FORWARD.

VISHY SAYS

5

LIGHTNING KID STRIKES

I earned my first rating from FIDE in 1984. This rating tells you about a chess player's skill level as calculated using a rating system called Elo. Named after its creator, Arpad Elo, a Hungarian American physics professor, it is a numerical value that indicates how strong a player is relative to other players.

I was starting to play in internationally rated events, but mostly in India before this. I was moving forward steadily and surely. My victory at the 1982 Tamil Nadu State Junior (Under-19) Championship held in Salem had the media watching me. It was around this time that they (notably chess journalist V. Kameswaran) began to call me 'Lightning Kid' – 'a little man in a big hurry' – for my speed and instinctive playing talent. I played very fast – and usually very well. I would often finish games in just 15–20 minutes, while my opponents might use up the whole clock. By 1983, when I was thirteen, I had been winning many local- and state-level championships in Tamil Nadu.

That year marked a milestone for me.

A STEP UP: AT THE SUB-JUNIOR CHESS CHAMPIONSHIP IN PANAJI, GOA

The National Sub-Junior Chess Championship was being held in Panaji, Goa. My mother's cousin, who lived there, played host to us when we went there for the tournament. A standout memory I have of the trip is of the food she served us, particularly a scrumptious vegetable au gratin that she had mastered from the popular cooking expert Tarla Dalal's recipe books.

The tournament turned out to be just as enjoyable, particularly my wins. I clinched the title with a perfect score of 9 out of 9 games. I began to get noticed on the national scene as this was my first major national-level win, and many began to call me a 'prodigy'. It wasn't something that went to my head, though – I was just keen on playing, and winning!

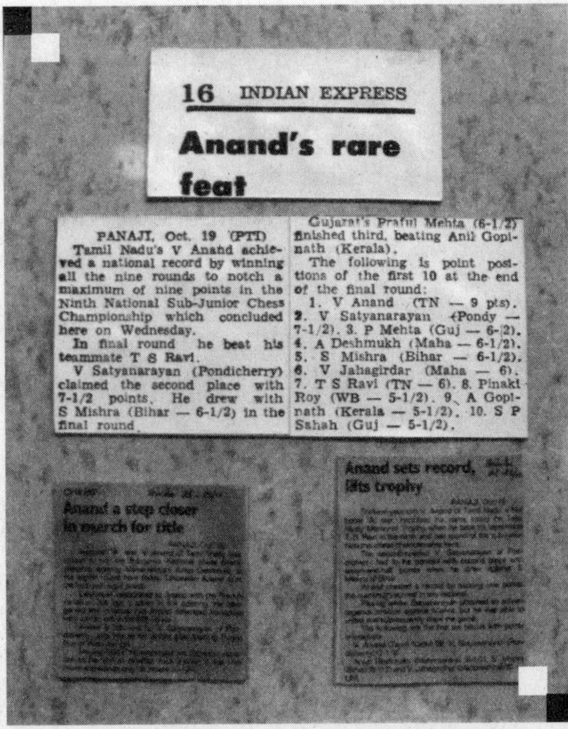

16 INDIAN EXPRESS

Anand's rare feat

PANAJI, Oct. 19 (PTI)

Tamil Nadu's V Anand achieved a national record by winning all the nine rounds to notch a maximum of nine points in the Ninth National Sub-Junior Chess Championship which concluded here on Wednesday.

In final round he beat his teammate T S Ravi.

V Satyanarayan (Pondicherry) claimed the second place with 7-1/2 points. He drew with S Mishra (Bihar — 6-1/2) in the final round.

Gujarat's Praful Mehta (6-1/2) finished third, beating Anil Gopinath (Kerala).

The following is point positions of the first 10 at the end of the final round:

1. V Anand (TN — 9 pts). 2. V Satyanarayan (Pondy — 7-1/2). 3. P Mehta (Guj — 6-1/2). 4. A Deshmukh (Maha — 6-1/2). 5. S Mishra (Bihar — 6-1/2). 6. V Jahagirdar (Maha — 6). 7. T S Ravi (TN — 6). 8. Pinaki Roy (WB — 5-1/2). 9. A Gopinath (Kerala — 5-1/2). 10. S P Sahah (Guj — 5-1/2).

Anand a step closer in march for title

Anand sets record, lifts trophy

WITH THE WIN IN GOA, I HIT THE HEADLINES FOR THE FIRST TIME

That year, I also defeated the nine-time national champion and my former tutor at the Tal Chess Club, Manuel Aaron, at the National Team Championship in Bombay (now Mumbai). It was the second time in two years that I'd pulled off a win against him, the first being in 1982 at the District Team Championship in Chennai.

The Indian Institute of Technology (IIT) Bombay campus in Powai played host to the national championship. Although the Madras District Chess

Association had taken the ambitious decision to field a team of promising teens from the state – the Madras Colts – they had no money to fund us. So, the renowned Indian playback singer S.P. Balasubrahmanyam stepped in and agreed to sponsor the team. For some reason, being quite innocent and a complete keen bean, I felt that I should offer up to Mr Balasubrahmanyam, as a token of thanks, the little money my mother had given me! Finally, I didn't go through with it.

During my game against Aaron, I was miserably sick, shaking with fever, and I turned up at the board swathed in woollens in the sultry heat of May. I ended up defeating him and won the top board prize. Aaron was a pioneer of chess in India and one of the best chess players in the country. This game was for me the starting point of a long, unbroken streak of success. I felt that I was ready to move forward to the next step. I gathered up all the opportunities and moved to a different stage.

Looking back, that win felt like all my hard work was beginning to show and shine. At the time, I was just happy to win – but now I realize how much it mattered then.

Before my sixteenth birthday I became the national champion, the youngest to do so yet.

***

In the following couple of years, I earned my IM norms, based on my performances, close at each other's heels. As mentioned earlier, the IM title in chess is the second-highest title, just below GM, awarded by FIDE. It's a permanent title – once an IM, always an IM!

I achieved my first IM norm at the 1984 Lloyds Bank Open tournament in London, my second IM norm at the Thessaloniki Olympiad in 1984 in Greece and the third norm in 1985 at the Asian Junior Championship in Hong Kong. I was recognized as an IM at the age of fifteen, making me the youngest Indian at the time to achieve the title and one among only a handful of IMs.

Though it wasn't something I was aware of or paying attention to, my rapid progress through the ranks of chess players was far ahead of anyone in Indian chess history. To earn the IM title, I performed strongly against international opposition in FIDE-rated events like the Asian Junior Championship. It showed I wasn't just dominating local players – I could compete at a high level globally.

At fifteen, showing steady results in tournaments was something usually seen in young Grandmasters from strong chess nations like the Soviet Union or Hungary. My IM title meant more than just an award – it showed that India finally had a world-class player ready to break past limits no one from the country had crossed before. I was playing – and beating – India's best senior players, most of whom were much older and more experienced, often in their late 20s and above.

With my win against Aaron, I firmly established myself as India's #1 player, not just a promising junior. It was quite clear now that my IM title and youth championships weren't flukes – I could beat top adult players consistently and confidently. This victory helped me get invitations to important international events, critical for earning GM norms. It added to my growing FIDE rating, making me a serious GM candidate.

I became India's hope for a true international contender in chess.

And that completely matched my own goals.

VISHY SAYS

WINNING IS RARELY ABOUT LUCK. IT'S ALMOST ALWAYS THE RESULT OF STEADY WORK, DISCIPLINE AND LEARNING FROM BOTH VICTORIES AND MISTAKES. EVEN SETBACKS OR CHALLENGES WHILE PLAYING STRONGER OPPONENTS CAN SHARPEN ONE'S SKILLS AND BUILD RESILIENCE.

OFTEN, PROGRESS ISN'T OBVIOUS IN THE MOMENT, BUT OVER TIME, THOSE SMALL IMPROVEMENTS ADD UP. ONE DAY, THE RESULTS START TO SHINE, SHOWING THAT ALL THE EFFORT AND PREPARATION HAVE BEEN WORTH IT. THAT'S THE REAL REWARD OF HARD WORK.

6

HOW LOSING HELPS YOU WIN

Our earliest lessons are imprinted on our minds and hearts. One of the things I learnt right at the start was something my mother insisted on: writing down my impressions immediately after a game, even a loss – in fact, especially if it was a defeat.

Initially, I was not keen to do this. It seemed like a bore. When I was young, like you are now, I didn't feel a pressing need to live up to a routine. I also tended to think that I would remember it all; or if it was a loss, I might not want to remember it ever! So, back then, I did it more for my mother's satisfaction than for my benefit. I would studiously and methodically write the notations down in neat letters and often underline – with a strong double stroke – the notes on the portions of the game where I had blundered.

As I grew older, this practice slowly grew on me. I began to see how it could help me improve by not making the same mistakes again. Writing things down right after losing – when I was still upset – actually helped me notice details I had missed. Not only did it help me spot my errors, but it also gave me the big picture – a 'macro' view. What if the things I had missed, the moves I did not make or did make, all fit into a sort of a worrying, 'losing' pattern that I needed to get rid of right away?

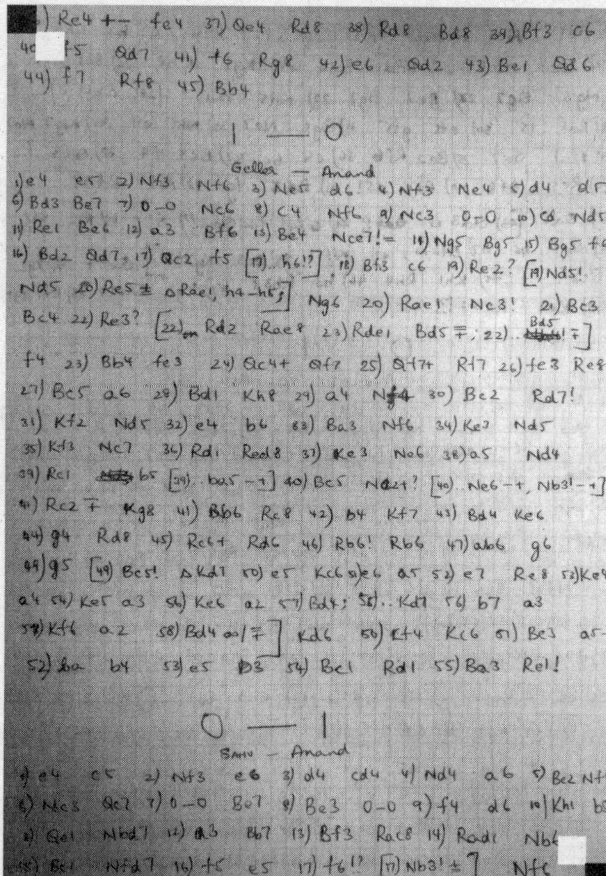
) Re4 +– fe4 37) Qe4 Rd8 38) Rd8 Bd8 39) Bf3 c6
40) f5 Qd7 41) f6 Rg8 42) e6 Qd2 43) Be1 Qd6
44) f7 Rf8 45) Bb4

1 — 0

Geller — Anand

1) e4 e5 2) Nf3 Nf6 3) Ne5 d6 4) Nf3 Ne4 5) d4 d5
6) Bd3 Be7 7) 0–0 Nc6 8) c4 Nf6 9) Nc3 0–0 10) c5 Nd5
11) Re1 Be6 12) a3 Bf6 13) Be4 Nce7!= 14) Ng5 Bg5 15) Bg5 f6
16) Bd2 Qd7 17) Qc2 f5 [17)...h6!?] 18) Bf3 c6 19) Re2? [19) Nd5!
Nd5 20) Re5 ± ΔRae1, h4–h5;] Ng6 20) Rae1 Nc3! 21) Bc3
Bc4 22) Re3? [22) on Rd2 Rae8 23) Rde1 Bd5 ∓; 22)... Bd5! ∓]
f4 23) Bb4 fe3 24) Qc4+ Qf7 25) Qf7+ Rf7 26) fe3 Re8
27) Bc5 a6 28) Bd1 Kh8 29) a4 Nf4 30) Bc2 Rd7!
31) Kf2 Nd5 32) e4 b6 33) Ba3 Nf6 34) Ke2 Nd5
35) Kf3 Nc7 36) Rd1 Red8 37) Ke3 Ne6 38) a5 Nd4
39) Rc1 b5 [39)...ba5 –+] 40) Bc5 Nc2+? [40)...Ne6 –+, Nb3! –+]
41) Rc2 ∓ Kg8 41) Bb6 Rc8 42) b4 Kf7 43) Bd4 Ke6
44) g4 Rd8 45) Rc6+ Rd6 46) Rb6! Rb6 47) ab6 g6
48) g5 [49) Bc5! ΔKd7 50) e5 Kc6 51) e6 a5 52) e7 Re8 53) Ke4
a4 54) Ke5 a3 55) Ke6 a2 57) Bd4; 56)...Kd7 56) b7 a3
57) Kf6 a2 58) Bd4 a1/∓] Kd6 50) Kf4 Kc6 51) Be3 a5 –+
52) ba b4 53) e5 b3 54) Bc1 Rd1 55) Ba3 Re1!

0 — 1

Sahu – Anand

1) e4 c5 2) Nf3 e6 3) d4 cd4 4) Nd4 a6 5) Be2 Nf6
6) Nc3 Qc7 7) 0–0 Be7 8) Be3 0–0 9) f4 d6 10) Kh1 b5
11) Qe1 Nbd7 12) a3 Bb7 13) Bf3 Rac8 14) Rad1 Nb6
15) Bc1 Nfd7 16) f5 e5 17) f6!? [17) Nb3! ±] Nf6

MY POST-GAME NOTES (PRETTY NEAT, RIGHT?) – MY MOTHER GOT ME INTO THIS HABIT AND I STILL FOLLOW IT, THOUGH IN ITS ABRIDGED VERSION

You may wonder if I always did the same after a win. Usually, following a victory, I would allow myself some room and stay away a little longer from writing down those notes. I was still curious to know if I played a line (which is a sequence of moves) in the best way possible, but the urge was not as strong as it was following defeats or missed opportunities. It was also a brilliant way to funnel my emotions after a game – anguish, remorse or regret (just kicking myself!) – and study the results objectively.

Once this practice became a habit, after every game I couldn't wait to revisit what I did or didn't do. I began to feel that without doing that, my understanding of my match experience was incomplete. The game was not just about winning or losing, but about how I had approached it and whether that was (or was not) the best way I could have played it in the circumstances.

Over time, I began widening the scope of my notes – jotting down my opponents' quirks, tendencies, gestures and all the little things that tended to distract me before or during a game. For instance, to caution myself against blitzing when I'm tense during a game, one of my notes reads:

> 'When you're almost winning and have more time than your opponent, DO NOT make a move. Pull your hand back. Get up, drink tea, wash your face, take a deep breath and then come back to the board.'

For rapid tie-breaks, I remind myself to roll up my sleeves so they don't hinder the speed of my movements on the board. I even have notes nudging myself to be more attentive to specific clues while playing against particular opponents. Armenian GM Levon Aronian, for one, had a habit of striking up a conversation on the morning of a game if he felt upbeat. It could just be playful banter about how he was going to give me a hard time. My self-scolding note for this kind of a situation says:

> 'Don't get into any small talk. Stop making jokes and pretending to be funny.'

Often, I'm amazed when I dig up these old notes and think, 'Wow, it seems to me now that I did everything beautifully...but at that moment, I was struggling, stuttering, hesitating and just generally hating myself.' At times, after games, I've been tired and put off scolding myself for later. But by the next morning, the intensity, the urge to do this properly – and make it useful for myself – is gone. What ends up as notes then is a summary of a summary, like a snack-sized version of a big dish. It's a hit-and-miss scenario, because delay only makes us forget details or think they are not important. All that the brief notes that I scribble with half a heart after a late breakfast the morning after a game tell me now is that I survived. So, really, the fresher the notes, the more useful they are. (That works for anything, anywhere, such as school and college too, but you already know that, right?)

My notes have served me well over the years as my go-to manual of sorts, reminding me of the pitfalls and the advantages I may come across. I used to revisit them often, particularly if I was returning to playing tournaments after a self-imposed break. Even if my notes aren't as detailed as they used to be, the habit is going strong.

And every time I go back to them, I remember: the best way to win is to understand how you lost.

VISHY SAYS

OBSERVING YOURSELF AND UNDERSTANDING YOUR MISTAKES IS A BIG STEP TOWARDS NOT MAKING THEM AGAIN. BUT FOR THAT, YOU MUST FIRST KNOW THAT YOU ARE MAKING AN ERROR. REVIEWING GAMES IS ALSO HOW ALL KINDS OF SPORTS COACHES HELP THEIR PLAYERS TO KNOW WHERE THEY MAY HAVE GONE WRONG AND HOW TO NOT MAKE THOSE MISTAKES AGAIN. YOU CAN START OFF BY DOING THIS YOURSELF.

7

GRANDMASTER

As a young player, the one title I passionately chased for two years was that of Grandmaster. Can you believe that India didn't have a GM then? No wonder that all my efforts revolved around that one giant dream!

It was both exciting and excruciating working towards that goal. At the Tata Steel Grandmaster Tournament in Calcutta in 1986, I missed my first GM norm by half a point, and at the Lloyds Bank Masters Open held later that year in London, it slipped away from me again by half a point. I was promoted to the top board and scored 7.5 points out of a possible 11 at the Chess Olympiad that year in Dubai, but a norm continued to be out of reach. There was no risk of failure involved in the pursuit, since no one had done it before in the country, but I still felt frustrated at missing it by the narrowest of margins.

Meanwhile, my competitive landscape had transformed. After the 1986 wins, I had quickly shifted focus to the international circuit. Before 1986, I had been building up my strengths on the national stage. Now I mostly competed in international super-tournaments. Stewart Reuben, a chess arbiter (an official who oversees

HOPEFUL, AT THE DUBAI CHESS OLYMPIAD IN 1986, WITH THE ENGLAND VERSUS POLAND GAMES GOING ON IN THE BACKGROUND

matches, enforces rules and resolves disputes to ensure a fair and smooth tournament), had in an earlier conversation in London given me advice: he had told me that it was possible that I would keep missing the norms for months and then suddenly turn into a GM almost effortlessly. I had doubted him then, but that's exactly how it happened.

Remember I told you about visiting the Baguio Convention Center in the Philippines when I was about ten, back when my father was posted there? That same hall was now the venue for the World Junior Chess Championship in July 1987! I was back – older, stronger and with something massive at stake.

The tournament had 52 players, including two GMs and 10 IMs. We were competing over 13 rounds in a format called the Swiss system – which basically meant that each round paired us based on how we had performed so far. So, the better you did, the tougher your next opponent. It was a bit like levelling up in a video game – win a round, and the next level got harder.

I didn't start off on fire. But then something clicked.

I beat Simen Agdestein of Norway, a GM and the top seed. That gave me a huge confidence boost. Then I won a crucial game against Vassily Ivanchuk, a brilliant and unpredictable player from Ukraine. Both wins were tough and tightly fought, and I felt like I was finally hitting my stride.

Going into the final round, I needed just half a point – a draw – to win the title. The last game was tense, and I played it carefully. When the draw was agreed, I knew I'd done it.

I had just become World Junior Chess Champion – and the first Indian ever to win that title.

***

Naturally, this marked an important milestone for Indian chess on the world stage. Initially, local media focused on Filipino and Soviet players. However, after my victory, I received a good amount of attention, with my games and interviews appearing prominently in the media in the Philippines. Back home too, my triumph was celebrated widely. I appeared on the covers of major magazines, including *The Illustrated Weekly*, and was hailed as a national hero.

It was India's first world junior title in chess, and it became a benchmark for later players.

Most importantly for me, this victory earned me my first GM norm.

Following this, at the Bhilwara International Chess Championship held in Delhi in late 1987, I picked up my second GM norm. My mother kept me away from distractions so that I wouldn't slip into my usual tendency to relax early when things were going my way and end up losing a game.

I finally won the title of Grandmaster with the third and final norm after a draw in the penultimate round at the Shakti Finance International Chess Tournament

MEETING THE THEN PRESIDENT OF INDIA, R. VENKATARAMAN, AT THE RASHTRAPATI BHAVAN IN 1988

in Coimbatore in 1987. The competitive field included five GMs and three other IMs – players such as Indians Pravin Thipsay, Ravi Hegde, Poorna Sharma Mithrakanth – and the Soviet GM Efim Geller. It was at this event that I clinched the final GM norm and I could hear Reuben's advice ringing in my ears.

That was how on 28 December 1987, just a few days after my 18th birthday, I became India's first Grandmaster (FIDE officially recognized this in March 1988).

When I finally earned that title, I wasn't just proud for myself. I was tickled pink that Indian chess had made it on to the world stage – and that now others could follow.

VISHY SAYS

IT ALWAYS MAKES SENSE TO KEEP WORKING AT A GOAL WITHOUT OBSESSING OVER HOW FAR YOU ARE FROM IT OR HOW HOPELESSLY YOU SEEM TO MISS THE MARK EACH TIME. IF YOU STICK TO CHASING IT, IT MIGHT EVENTUALLY BE YOURS – AND EVEN WHEN PROGRESS FEELS INVISIBLE, EACH EFFORT LEAVES YOU BETTER PREPARED FOR SUCCESS.

8

ON BECOMING A CHAMPION

The most important thing is to keep learning from your experiences. Everything you go through – good or bad – shapes who you are. In fact, you learn the most when something doesn't go your way. Maybe you got impatient, maybe you felt frustrated, or maybe life just surprised you. Even if you plan everything perfectly, sometimes things can still go wrong.

That's why it helps to step back and look at yourself as if you were your own rival. Ask: What did I miss? What can I do better next time? Champions are not afraid to be honest with themselves. Improving is harder than it looks, but it starts with being curious and asking 'why'. If you can explain to yourself what went wrong, you're already halfway to fixing it.

A CHAMPION IS SIMPLY SOMEONE WHO NEVER STOPS LEARNING.

VISHY SAYS

9

LUCK ON MY SIDE

Looking back, I realize that I was incredibly lucky throughout this time. I don't mean fluky-lucky in the sense of winning games by chance – but in being in the right place at the right time. Especially when I had to make big decisions.

Teenagers in sports careers have studies to juggle with their rigorous physical (or mental) schedules. Alongside, they may hesitate to invest time and effort entirely in sport because, naturally, they fear falling behind their peers in studies. Is the risk worth the reward? – they may wonder.

In my case, the breaks I needed to get ahead in my chess career somehow came at well-timed moments when I would have had to weigh my options anyway – I became the national champion in the tenth standard, and GM two years later when I was leaving school and getting ready for college. I was ranked fifth in the world when I finished my bachelor's degree in commerce. The long and complex process of deciding between a dedicated sporting career and higher studies, which my peers obsessed over, often painfully, was something I didn't have to get into.

I think that if you lose yourself completely and entirely in a sports career at too young an age, it is easy to miss the big picture. It could make relating to different people, situations and even everyday living quite challenging. To keep a balance and to not put everything into one basket – physically, emotionally, mentally and intellectually – it's best to find a hobby or a pastime removed from your sport. For me it was astronomy or studying the sciences and maths.

Come to think of it, it's a lot like our school holidays as I remember them. The day after school heads into a summer break, you're madcap-crazy with joy, but if you don't engage your brain in some way soon enough, it begins to feel boring and less like a holiday. After two weeks of your holiday, when you still have six weeks left, each day feels like every other day and time just drags. If you have hobbies to enjoy, the days seem to happily disappear.

Similarly, in chess, it's much easier to take your mind off a painful defeat or a run of poor form if you find other things to do that are fun and make you happy. It's difficult if chess is all you know and if all your joy depends on it. An unforgettable example of this was the brilliant American chess player, Bobby Fischer.

Fischer started playing at six, and by his teens, he was one of the best players in the world. In 1972, at age twenty-nine, he became World Champion by defeating Boris Spassky of the Soviet Union. But Bobby didn't just play chess, he was obsessed with it. He studied it for hours every day and didn't enjoy much else. He wanted to be in control of everything around his chess-playing. He made unusual demands during tournaments, like adjusting the lighting or moving the cameras, and sometimes refused to play unless everything was just right. After winning the world title, he stopped playing publicly. He didn't trust people, believed that others were cheating, and went into a shell. In 1992, he returned for one final public match, then retreated again.

As chess players, we have all learnt as many lessons from his life as from his games – both inspiring and instructive. His chess is hard not to admire, and he made it possible for players after him to become chess professionals and make a living from playing the game. In many ways, we stand on the shoulders of greats such as him. But his life was also a warning against doing only one thing and nothing else.

In comparison, I believe my journey in the sport to be much easier and without the kind of pressure someone like Fischer probably had. In his time, he really had to give up *everything* to become a chess player.

I didn't.

The world around us – our environment – shapes how our brain works, what we enjoy and how we grow those interests. The first time you learn about something, and the place or mood you're in, can make a big difference to how you feel about it later. I wasn't browbeaten into picking up chess or playing it. My parents left it to me to divide my time between my studies and chess. Their attitude freed up my mind and put me at ease, and helped me to fall back on either, as it suited me.

Chess for me had no pangs or pressure tied to it.

And yet what a mixed bag it was!

Luck may havc brought me to important moments, but what really shaped me was what came after – the quiet time when I had to face my wins and losses honestly, understand what they meant and figure out how to grow. Success or failure didn't just disappear once the game ended. Instead, each result left a mark. You might think that winning the GM title would put me on top of the world forever, but that's not how it was…

VISHY SAYS

LOVE YOUR MAIN PASSION, BUT DON'T MAKE IT THE *ONLY* THING IN YOUR LIFE. IF YOU PLAY A SPORT, PAINT OR CODE ALL DAY, EVERY DAY, AND NOTHING ELSE, IT'S EASY TO BURN OUT OR FEEL STUCK.

HOBBIES AREN'T A DISTRACTION – THEY REFRESH YOUR MIND, GIVE YOU NEW IDEAS AND KEEP YOU HAPPY EVEN WHEN YOUR MOST IMPORTANT PURSUIT GETS TOUGH. WHEN YOU STAY BALANCED, YOU RETURN TO YOUR SPORT OR SKILL OR OTHER PASSION WITH MORE ENERGY, SHARPER FOCUS AND A CLEARER HEAD. IN THE LONG RUN, THIS BALANCE IS YOUR SUPERPOWER.

10

WHEN THE PIECES SETTLE

You'd think I'd have stayed on cloud nine for ages after becoming GM. Of course it was thrilling, but strangely enough, after being in seventh heaven at winning the title, I went through something I hadn't expected at all. It was my first taste of what happens after chasing a dream. Once I reached it, I didn't know what to do next. It's like when you've been studying for months for exams or training for a big match, and then – *poof* – it's over. You're happy, but also oddly empty, like a balloon that floated high and then popped.

I had been fully focused on my goal. But once I achieved it, I kept looking back instead of setting new ones. Tournaments and scores no longer excited me, and my performance suffered. For six months, I just moved along without any real progress, stuck in the same place.

I kept playing, though, and that's what led me to the answer. While travelling for tournaments and talking to other Grandmasters, I realized I wasn't alone – many players went through this phase. Sometimes when a goal is so big and takes up all your energy, you don't know what to aim for once you've done it. Slowly, I was able to get back on track, just in time.

Because the next phase of my life as a chess player was about to begin.

***

Before 1991, I spent a lot of time flying between India and Europe for tournaments. Airports, hotels, repeat. I thought it would be smart to have a base in Europe – it would save money, cut travel time and make it easier to get invited to tournaments at short notice. Back then, remember, there were fewer flights, and you couldn't just pull out your phone to book a ticket or a hotel. Organizers abroad often assumed I wouldn't show up because it was too far. However, if I were already in Europe, that would change.

I almost moved to Amsterdam, where my friend Albert Toby lived. But then something happened that made me rethink my plans.

I ran into a fresh set of parents at the Linares International Chess Tournament in February 1991.

'What?!' I can hear you wondering.

Well, it happened like this.

At the 1991 Linares tournament, I met an elderly couple – Mauricio 'Maurice' Perea and his wife, Nieves – who were big fans of chess and football. Linares was a small mining town in southern Spain, but its chess tournament was well on its way to becoming legendary.

In the round robin tournament (where everyone plays everyone else), I took up little time on my clock, my hands whirring over the board as I made my moves at blinding speed against Estonian American GM, Jaan Ehlvest, in round 4. Maurice watched, first bewildered, then curious if my clock was working at all, since it had barely taken any time. During one of my games, I was playing so fast that Maurice actually walked over to check if my clock was broken!

The game ended in a draw, and Maurice invited me over for dinner that evening. As I chomped on the yummy food, Maurice gave me 'serious' advice: to slow down and think more during games. With a tiny grin, I cheekily replied, 'Okay, Maurice, how about I take a minute more next time?' He laughed and hugged me. His wife Nieves fished a promise out of me that I would take her out to the best Chinese restaurant in town if I beat one of the top guys (which wasn't a risk, since Chinese food joints in Linares at the time were not exactly five-star).

That dinner was the start of a warm, family-like bond. Maurice and Nieves welcomed me into their home in Collado Mediano, a mountain town in northwest Spain. Nieves fussed over me – cooking for me, mending my clothes, even doing my laundry. Maurice, on the other hand, was baffled by my fashion and music choices. I would typically have on a pair of large white sneakers, my hands stuffed in the pockets of my baggy jeans. I would be listening to the Irish rock band the Cranberries (know 'Zombie'?) or the British synth-pop duo the Pet Shop Boys (how about 'It's a Sin'?) on my Walkman

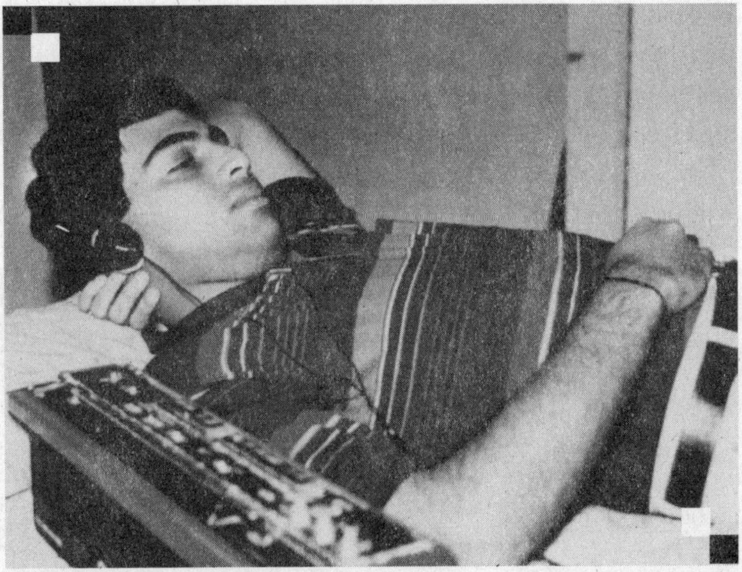

MY FAVOURITE MUSIC RANGED FROM THE PET SHOP BOYS TO THE BEE GEES

(a then revolutionary portable audio player that used 'cassette tapes' of music). For Maurice, who was an Englishman and a passionate devotee of Beethoven and Brahms, both my clothes and the music I headbanged to were beyond comprehension. His favourite refrain was '*Caramba que ese so!* What is this noise?', referring to my music (isn't that totally like all parents!). Maurice also never stopped wondering aloud about my insistence on drizzling ketchup over my pasta (I have now progressed to whole-wheat spaghetti with seafood, and without ketchup, if you please!).

Despite all the things we did differently, Maurice and I were bound by a love of history, astronomy and, of course, chess. One of my unforgettable memories is of us lounging in patio chairs on the deck of their beautiful, sprawling five-bedroom home, inhaling the scent of ferns, cypress and the earth, and watching the sun disappear behind the mountains on the horizon.

It was Maurice who bought me my first fine jacket – a checkered grey single-breasted piece from the Alta Moda boutique in Linares. Warm, affectionate and fatherly, he said, 'Vishy, you're not just a chess player anymore. You're a future World Champion. You should now start dressing like one.'

It was, then, up to me to go from dressing like one to becoming one!

VISHY SAYS

WHEN YOU FINALLY REACH A BIG GOAL, IT'S TEMPTING TO SIT BACK AND ENJOY IT FOREVER. BUT THE TRUTH IS, IF YOU STOP MOVING FORWARD, YOU CAN QUICKLY FEEL STUCK. SUCCESS ISN'T THE END OF THE ROAD – IT'S A NEW STARTING POINT.

THE TRICK IS TO SET FRESH GOALS RIGHT AWAY, EVEN SMALL ONES, SO THAT YOUR MIND STAYS EXCITED AND ACTIVE. AND DON'T GO IT ALONE – SPEND TIME WITH PEOPLE WHO PUSH YOU TO DO BETTER AND KEEP YOU CURIOUS. THAT WAY, YOU'LL KEEP LEARNING, GROWING AND FINDING NEW REASONS TO LOVE WHAT YOU DO.

11

ON FAILING

Failure stings. It can feel like the world is watching, disappointed, while you carry the weight of having let yourself down, and others too. At times, it even brings panic and self-doubt. Yet in sport, as in life, you cannot run from failure. You have to pause, steady yourself and search within for the strength to begin again. It helps to remember that nearly everyone faces moments like these. Failure doesn't mean the end of your story – it's just a difficult chapter that teaches you something new about who you are and what you're capable of.

No one succeeds alone. I was fortunate to lean on my mother, my coaches and my close friends. Their encouragement, together with the lessons I gathered from my experiences, gave me the courage to face difficult moments head-on. Sometimes a few encouraging words or a bit of friendly advice can make a big difference. They remind you that you're not alone and that there's always someone cheering you on when things get tough.

There is no single cure for failure. Each setback demands its own response. You have to adapt, to adjust, to keep chiselling away until you break through. The hardest step is to admit you have failed; the next is to confront it directly. From there, it is a matter of patient, determined effort – taking one clear step after another until the obstacle is overcome.

As the saying reminds us: it is not over until it is over. In sport especially, every defeat carries within it the seed of a stronger return.

FAILURE ISN'T THE END – IT'S PART OF THE PATH THAT LEADS YOU FORWARD.

VISHY SAYS

12

THE MEMORY MYSTERY...SOLVED

What's the last thing you forgot? Your lunchbox? A maths formula? Where you left your phone charger? You might think a chess player never forgets – that we're supposed to be walking memory machines, capable of holding in our heads a thousand moves, hundreds of positions and more than 50 years of chess history. But let me tell you a secret that will take me right off that cerebral pedestal: in January 1998, right in the middle of my World Championship match against Anatoly Karpov in Lausanne, Switzerland, I forgot my own wedding anniversary.

Yes, you read that correctly. A date that most people would etch into their memory forever had somehow slipped right out of mine.

This was the age of three-and-a-half-inch floppy disks – those black, squarish information storage devices that stored data before CDs were developed. If you've never seen one, ask someone older...or, for more fun, google why they were called 'floppy' in the first place!

Every night during the match, whatever preparation work my team and I had done would be saved on these floppies and stored in a safe. My wife, Aruna, would lock them away herself.

One night, after putting away the disks, she turned to me with a knowing smile and told me that the code to unlock the safe was easy to recall – 2706.

Confused, I said, 'That's a silly code… Which player has a rating like that?' Live Elo ratings weren't around then, and ratings were usually updated to a difference of five, so 2706 didn't seem realistic! Aruna's expression changed instantly from sweet to frozen. 'It's not anyone's rating,' she said coldly. 'It's our wedding anniversary.'

I had the world's stupidest look on my face. We were only in our second year of marriage, and here I was, struggling to connect the dots between a four-digit code and the most important date in our shared calendar. (Share this with your parents, and they might tell you why it's the kind of mistake I could never live down.)

The truth is, for all the moves, games and notations I can recall at will, I'm just as capable as anyone else of forgetting something obvious – especially if it's outside my usual zone of focus. Most chess players can replay a game they played 20 years ago, move for move, but ask them to recite a five-item grocery list and you'll see panic flash across their faces.

Back then, before the internet became our collective memory and before mobile phones began beeping reminders at us, we relied on the people around us for prompts. A spouse, a teammate, a coach – they were our human alarms. Now, we're hunched over devices, thumbs scrolling and swiping, with Google popping up reminders about flights, birthdays and dinner reservations.

***

People often assume chess players have 'eidetic' or photographic memory, but the reality is far less magical – and a lot more interesting. In fact, the Dutch psychologist and chess player Adriaan de Groot proved decades ago that our memory advantage isn't about storing perfect snapshots in our heads.

In one of his famous experiments, de Groot showed four groups of players – Grandmasters, Masters, experts and class 'A' players – a chessboard with 22 pieces in a real game position. Then he asked them to recreate it. Grandmasters and Masters did astonishingly well, reproducing 93 per cent of the positions correctly. Experts managed 72 per cent and class 'A' players 51 per cent.

But here's the twist: when the same pieces were placed randomly, with no logic or structure, everyone – including the Grandmasters – collapsed to recalling just three or four pieces correctly.

The lesson? We don't memorize piece-by-piece; we memorize patterns. We see familiar shapes, pawn structures and tactical ideas. Our minds chunk them together into meaningful units, the same way a musician doesn't remember every note individually but sees entire chords and phrases.

It's like showing an artist a landscape. They will remember the red boat with its name painted in white, the little chapel by the river, the backdrop of mountains and trees. But if you move everything around – remove the chapel, break the boat, add 20 random objects – even the artist will struggle to recreate the scene.

When I remember a chess position, it's a bit like telling myself a story: 'These three pawns haven't moved… White's bishop is here – I've seen this in a Nimzo-Indian opening… The pawn structure should be like this, except one pawn is out of place.' The key is that the picture makes sense to me. If it doesn't, my recall may be no better than anyone else's.

In my younger days, I could remember every move from every game I played. As years went by and the number of games, openings and variations multiplied, my brain adapted. I stopped storing every detail and started keeping the important markers – the opening choice, a critical mistake, a surprising tactic.

The same thing happened with phone numbers. As a teenager, I could rattle off dozens from memory. Now, if my phone battery dies, I'm basically stranded – unless the person I need to call is someone I'm close to like my mother, Aruna or an old friend whose number I learnt in the 90s. That part of my memory has simply gone rusty from lack of use.

Pattern memory shows up in fun ways too. At simultaneous exhibitions, where I play 20 or more amateurs at once, I don't carry every board position in my head. Instead, I store a few key snippets: which boards I'm ahead on, which ones are tricky and which ones need urgent attention. If I walk past and a piece is missing, I can often tell immediately – not because I remember the exact position, but because the 'harmony' of the board feels off.

Sometimes I'll call a player out: 'Hey, put back my piece.' Other times, if the missing piece doesn't change much, I'll let it go. And if it somehow improves my position? Well…let's just say I'm not in a hurry to correct the error.

In tournaments, remembering a move isn't enough; you have to remember *why* you made it. When I'm

A PHOTOSHOOT IN 1998

sure of a move's purpose, I play it confidently. When I only have a vague sense it might work, I approach it cautiously, double-checking my reasoning. Often, it's a process of elimination – ruling out moves I know are wrong until the best candidate remains.

That's why I constantly revise and refresh my lines. In World Championship prep, my team would stage training camps months in advance. We'd sometimes bring in an 'outsider' to test me with unfamiliar moves. Ahead of my matches in Mexico (2007), Bonn (2008) and Sofia (2010), a teenage Magnus Carlsen came to train with me – his fresh perspective helped me to remember and adapt at high speed.

Whether it's sparring with Magnus Carlsen or remembering a grocery list, I've learnt memory isn't magic – it's about practice, patterns and perspective. And if I forget my anniversary once in a while... well, that's what stories – and forgiveness – are for, right?

VISHY SAYS

MEMORY ISN'T ONLY ABOUT REMEMBERING EVERYTHING PERFECTLY. IT'S ALSO ABOUT RECOGNIZING PATTERNS AND UNDERSTANDING THE BIG PICTURE. PRACTICE AND CONTEXT – UNDERSTANDING HOW THINGS CONNECT IN DIFFERENT SITUATIONS – HELP YOU REMEMBER WHAT TRULY MATTERS. AND IF YOU FORGET SOMETHING IMPORTANT SOMETIMES, DON'T WORRY – THAT'S JUST PART OF BEING HUMAN.

13

ARUNA, MY TOP TEAMMATE

When you think of chess, you probably imagine one player sitting across from another, deep in thought, moving pieces on a board. It looks like a completely solo game. But let me tell you a secret: I've had a long-time teammate – my wife, Aruna.

When we got married in 1996, she began travelling with me to tournaments. At first, it looked like she was just coming along for company. But very quickly, I realized she was taking on so much more. She came from an advertising background and was good at handling people, besides being more organized than me in many ways. She handled the tickets, the hotels, the schedules, and even the endless meetings and official events that come with top tournaments. All those little things can tire a player out before even reaching the board. With her taking care of them, I could focus fully on the game.

But it wasn't just about the logistics. Aruna also understood me in a way no coach or second could. If I lost a tough game, she knew when to leave me alone with my thoughts and when to pull me out of a gloomy mood. If I won, she would celebrate, but she also reminded me not to get carried away because the tournament wasn't over yet. That balance made a huge difference.

During the intense World Championship matches, when the pressure was crushing, she was always calm. I could rely on her steady presence to keep me grounded. I often joked that she became my 'filter'. Everyone wanted my time – organizers, media, even fans – but she made sure I wasn't distracted or exhausted. She protected my mental space, which was as important as any preparation I did on the chessboard.

ARUNA, MY BEST FRIEND, TEAMMATE AND CHEERLEADER

So yes, I'm the one people see at the board, but Aruna has been part of every victory. She has truly been my strongest teammate.

VISHY SAYS

SUCCESS MAY LOOK LIKE A ONE-PERSON SHOW, BUT BEHIND IT THERE'S OFTEN SOMEONE QUIETLY SUPPORTING, ENCOURAGING AND HELPING YOU STAY STRONG. NEVER FORGET TO VALUE YOUR TEAMMATES – EVEN IN GAMES THAT SEEM LIKE THEY ARE PLAYED ALONE.

14

THE MEMORY VAULT

You might be wondering, after chapter 12, what really goes on with this memory business. How much does a chess player need to have at instant recall, and how much can be tucked away for later use? Let me take you back to one event and show you the picture. That's the thing about memory in chess – it's not just about remembering a billion moves. It's about remembering the right one at the right moment.

It was during a big tournament – the kind where every half-point matters, and preparation can mean the difference between a good showing and an early ticket home. On the morning of a game, after breakfast, my team of four trainers (or 'seconds') and I would spend hours debating final choices and lines. Trainers or seconds are trusted assistants, often strong chess players or analysts, who help a player prepare for and compete in tournaments, particularly high-stakes ones. A 'line', as I mentioned earlier, means a specific sequence of moves, a path of play, that could be followed during a game. It can be a single, continuous series of moves or a branch within a game where players go on to different move choices. Think of it as a pathway the player could take through the game, and each separate sequence of moves creates a new 'line'.

My team would make me to go over my notes before breaking off to get back to work while I showered and took a nap. In the final 45-minute stretch before heading off to the venue, I would sit at the board in the training room while my seconds stood around me, forming a half-moon and, by turns, throw positions at me to solve. If I was unable to solve a position in the third or fourth attempt and they were all standing around me, perhaps secretly wondering how I ever became a World Champion, the embarrassment and burn I felt was intense. If a similar position popped up in a game, I would never be in doubt anymore – the disgrace I'd experienced earlier would remind me instantly of what I should have done, of what I could now do. Sometimes having your ego take a knock before a game is a good thing. You are then a lot sharper at the board.

The rule of thumb for remembering deeply is to look at a position once, then not look at it for a day, then go over it once again and skip it for three days, and then go back and look at it yet again. By the eighth time you've looked at it, your brain has already encoded the memory, and every time you come back to it, it only gets reinforced.

In later years, what I often did was take photographs of all the positions I wanted to revise and kept them on my phone. When I was on a flight or free at another time, I flipped through them. The idea was to expose my brain to what I want it to recall. It's helpful to revise the position or idea a month later, repeat the same after three more months and by the end of the year it should have set up camp in your brain. The only guarantee to remembering is periodic revision (hmm, yes, your teachers are right about that!).

Even the things we know inside out are worth refreshing. It's like travelling back in time and remembering almost everything associated with a childhood photo when it is shown to you. It brings back recollections of the occasion when it was taken, what the setting was and even the emotions felt at the time. In chess, a lot of the work involves going over positions, lines, variations and ideas we already know, so we are essentially repeating our notes to ourselves.

Once I establish an emotional connect with a particular pattern, it makes it harder to forget. My memory of positions and lines is much stronger if the reason for remembering them is interesting – a game connected to a painful loss, perhaps, or if something is new and interesting. If, as an example, I've experienced a crushing rook ending and lost a game, the next time I walk into a rook ending I will probably feel my hair stand on end and a trickle of sweat run down my back, because the memory of that distressing defeat suddenly comes alive.

I still remember playing Hungarian grandmaster Judit Polgár, one of the strongest players in the world. She banged out her moves so quickly it was like she'd played this exact game before. She hadn't – but the position was close enough to one she had studied and her brain was on autopilot.

No two games were ever alike, which suits me perfectly. That's the thing about chess: history doesn't repeat exactly, but it rhymes. Positions come back in slightly different shapes. If you've seen something like it before, your mind says, *Hang on – I know this tune!* And that tune can lead you straight to the right move.

You have to keep revising your notes, run a check on your approaches through modern chess engines or computer programs that analyse positions and try newer paths.

Once in a while, you may run into the same conclusions – a position that is good for Black, for instance – but by not approaching them through hackneyed methods your knowledge of it becomes more sophisticated. If I start working on a new problem in the morning, by the evening I may discover 20 ways to tackle it. These approaches will remain fresh in my head for at least a week afterwards. If one of them happens to be similar to a different position I worked on two months ago, that adds itself on to the fresh learning. In effect, it's learning an old lesson a new way. Anything on the board that offers you two or three approaches to remembering it improves your chances.

However, if the attempt is to cram a multitude of positions and lines into your memory without knowing which one to remember with the greatest intensity, it can always catch you unawares. The one thing you didn't check could be the one thing that crops up on the board. If I haven't revised my notes, the chances of me forgetting my preparation runs high. It's why my team's chorus cry for me during a World Championship is 'Revise, revise, revise.'

***

I wouldn't really brag about my memory to do with things outside of chess. I'm quite terrible with faces. Before a school reunion, I usually go through Facebook for recent pictures of my former classmates, so I don't embarrass myself. I'm also known for forgetting start timings of tournaments. At the 1995 Intel Rapid Chess Grand Prix tournament in Paris, in what was supposed to be my first game against Russian GM Garry Kasparov after our World Championship match that year, I jumbled up the start time. It didn't work in my favour that I had confused *trois* (3 p.m.) and *treize* (thirteen, 1300 hours) in French. I should have simply clarified the time in English. I walked into the hall only in time to play the second game, and that too because I'd decided to get there early to settle in!

It's similar with pairings. I don't forget pairings if I know the pairing numbers and can even reel off the pairings of an entire tournament. Pairing means the process of assigning opponents to players in a tournament. It involves determining who will play against whom in each round, based on various factors like current score, rating and colour preference.

Often, I'll go up to the arbiter and inquire what the time control of the tournament I'm playing is. It's not that I've forgotten. It could well be a blitz tournament, but since the current tendency is to bunch tournaments in a group, it can get tough to remember, especially when the last three played were under different time controls.

I tend to remember alpha-numeric airport boarding gates according to chess opening codes. With books I've read or movies I've recently watched, I might be able to lay a finger on the storyline and the main characters, but the title may escape me. Often, I've checked out of a hotel, leaving my mouse pad behind. Here, the problem was not that I didn't remember that I had brought a mouse pad along, but that the mouse pad was something I saw lying on the table every day and it just blended in with the furniture. That made it difficult to stay memorable.

I've also been guilty of misplacing at least half a dozen gemstone rings that I wore at my mother's insistence, because she had faith they would bring me luck. Of course, it was only the jeweller who had a good run of fortune as the precious stones kept growing in size and value each time I lost one. Tired of my repeated carelessness, she eventually gave up buying them.

But I never gave up on one important thing – wanting to keep learning.

In the end, memory isn't magic. It's a muscle. You train it with repetition, you feed it with curiosity and sometimes you laugh at it when it fails you. The mouse pads, gemstone rings and wrong start times will come and go. But the lessons – the ones drilled in by embarrassment, hard work and the occasional lucky escape – those tend to stick. And that's why, whether

I'm chasing a new idea on the board or learning from an old mistake, my team's favourite advice still applies: *revise, revise, revise.*

If memory can be trained, I figured, then I'd just keep training it. That's one thing I never stopped doing – and still haven't.

VISHY SAYS

MEMORY ISN'T ABOUT STORING EVERYTHING AT ONCE – IT'S ABOUT TRAINING YOUR BRAIN TO RECALL THE RIGHT THING AT THE RIGHT MOMENT. REPETITION, REVISION AND CONNECTING EMOTIONS TO WHAT YOU LEARN MAKE MEMORIES STICK. AND IN CASE YOU FORGET, JUST LAUGH IT OFF AND KEEP TRAINING!

15

BRAINY STUFF YOU SHOULD KNOW ABOUT

Sometimes in chess, the strangest ideas pop into your head at exactly the right moment. What's amazing is that these thoughts often don't come from situations that look even a little similar to the one you are actually playing. It's as if your brain has a secret way of pulling out something you learnt long ago and applying it like magic, even when the pieces on the board don't line up the same way.

I remember one time when I was chatting with Ukrainian GM Vassily Ivanchuk – he's a genius both on and off the board – about an opening called the Catalan. He showed me a beautiful little trick. Black attacks White's queen, but instead of defending it right away, White calmly moves a bishop. This surprising move makes the queen's attack backfire badly. Black ends up stuck with two terrible options. If Black moves the queen away, White wins a rook and a bishop, which is a big material gain. But if Black tries to keep the material balanced, the pieces get so awkwardly placed that the position becomes hopeless anyway.

Fast forward about a month, and I'm playing American GM Joel Benjamin at the 1989 Wijk aan Zee tournament. We're in the Sicilian Defence – an opening that looks completely different from the Catalan. But suddenly, something clicks in my mind. I think, 'Hey! This looks just like that Ivanchuk trick!' Even though the position on the board was totally different, the same basic idea worked perfectly. This time, I wasn't just getting some compensation – I was actually winning material (you know, of course, that in chess 'winning material' means capturing your opponent's pieces so that you have more or stronger pieces than they do).

Joel was caught completely off guard, and the game swung in my favour.

AT THE HOOGOVENS TOURNAMENT IN WIJK AAN ZEE IN 1989

Moments like these make you realize something important: new things you learn, even if you don't use them right away, can sneak back into your life when you least expect it. You might think, 'Why bother learning this if I don't need it now?' But your brain stores all kinds of ideas and information, and later on, these can suddenly come together in a winning move.

For decades, scientists have been studying how the human brain works. One famous idea is that the left side of your brain is better at logic and language, while the right side handles pictures and patterns. Because chess seems all about calculation and logic, many people assume it's a 'left-brain' activity. But it's not that simple. I've found that emotions play a huge role too. When I'm playing against someone I really don't want to lose to, my brain seems sharper. I spot things I might have missed otherwise, and I fight harder.

The truth is, our brains are amazing at making connections between completely different things – but only if we give them enough variety to work with. If you only study one thing, your brain's connections stay narrow. But if you explore lots of different ideas, even ones that seem unrelated, your mind starts to see patterns and links that others miss.

That's why sometimes I like to study openings that I don't even plan to use in my next game. I'm just curious about them. For instance, I once spent time going through the games of Russian GM Vladimir Kramnik and Belarusian Israeli GM Boris Gelfand, focusing on the Leningrad Variation of the Grünfeld Defence. It was far from my usual style. I didn't expect much to come from it, but over time, little details from those games popped into my mind during totally different positions. I came up with ideas my opponent hadn't thought about, and suddenly the initiative was mine.

Our brains store so much more than we realize, and if we keep feeding them with interesting things, they reward us with surprises when we need them most.

And this isn't just true for chess. The late Steve Jobs, the founder of Apple, once told a story from his college days that shows exactly how this works. He dropped out of his main courses but wandered into a calligraphy class – the art of producing beautiful handwriting using a brush or a special pen – taught by a former Trappist monk. It had nothing to do with computers or electronics, which he was supposed to be studying. But years later, when Apple was building the first Macintosh computer, all that calligraphy knowledge came flooding back. That's why the Mac was the first computer to have multiple fonts and beautiful spacing between letters. If Jobs hadn't taken that class on a whim, computer design might have stayed boring and clunky-looking for much longer.

Jobs used to say, 'You can't connect the dots looking forward; you can only connect them looking backwards.' You never know when something you learn today will turn out to be exactly what you need years later.

So, here's my advice: explore things just for fun, not only for instant results. That book you pick up on a whim, the guitar lessons you try out or the weekend language class you take just because you're curious – they might all add up to something amazing down the road.

For me, a random curiosity about an opening I didn't even play regularly ended up winning me a serious game. For Steve Jobs, a calligraphy class shaped the look of modern computers. The dots don't always connect right away, but when they do, they can change everything.

But the dots may not connect when you most want them to. The next part of my journey wasn't all about happy surprises and lucky moments. In chess – and in life – things don't always go your way. Sometimes the board is stormy, and you end up on the losing side. Those moments test you in ways nothing else can, and how you respond to defeat is where the real lessons begin.

VISHY SAYS

LEARNING ISN'T JUST ABOUT WHAT YOU NEED RIGHT NOW – IT'S ABOUT FILLING YOUR BRAIN WITH IDEAS AND PATTERNS THAT CAN SURPRISE YOU LATER. EXPLORE WIDELY, STAY CURIOUS AND TRUST THAT EVEN SEEMINGLY UNRELATED KNOWLEDGE CAN CONNECT IN UNEXPECTED WAYS TO HELP YOU WIN – OR SOLVE PROBLEMS – DOWN THE LINE.

16

LEARNING TO LEARN

The ability to learn is one of the most important qualities you can have. In school, you study many subjects and pick up different skills, but perhaps the biggest lesson school gives you is this: learning itself matters. Learning can be fun too! Every time you try something new, whether it's solving a puzzle, drawing or playing a game, you're giving your brain a chance to grow. Even small discoveries, small things you learn for the first time, count and can make you feel proud.

Knowledge isn't fixed, like a picture hanging on a wall. It's alive, always growing, always changing. That's why it helps to stay curious, to keep asking questions, to be willing to try again and to adapt when things don't go as planned.

In chess especially, one quality makes all the difference – objectivity. This means being able to look at yourself the way others see you and to judge your own work honestly. It's not always easy, but it's powerful. It allows you to notice mistakes and, more importantly, to correct them. Every defeat on the board is really a message: something wasn't understood, something wasn't done right. If you don't face it yourself, your opponent will point it out for you – often very clearly!

VISHY SAYS

REAL LEARNING BEGINS WITH OBJECTIVITY – IT SHOWS YOU WHAT TO CHANGE AND HOW TO GROW.

17

WIN SOME, LOSE SOME

It was the early hours of 19 July 2001, just a day after I'd lost to Russian GM Alexander Morozevich in round six of the Dortmund Sparkassen Chess Meeting. I lay awake in our hotel room, watching the first soft streaks of sunlight brush the curtains. My breath rose and fell in heavy waves. My eyelids were so tired, but my brain refused to sleep. My head felt like it weighed a hundred pounds, and dark swirls of thought kept spinning around one single idea: *I hate chess.*

All I could see was Morozevich's grin as he shook my hand and called my loss a 'birthday present' for him. I had won the World Championship in Tehran just seven months earlier. Now I looked completely exhausted, with three draws, two losses, and almost sure to finish at the bottom of the tournament.

Dortmund, a German city with a strong love for chess, was hosting six of the top ten Super Grandmasters. The line-up included Russian GM Vladimir Kramnik, Bulgarian GM Veselin Topalov, Hungarian GM Peter Leko, Morozevich, English GM Michael Adams and me.

It was an invite-only, double round-robin tournament, meaning that each player faced the others twice. Many people saw it as a test for the new world champions: Kramnik, who had famously beaten Kasparov in 2000, and me, the FIDE champion.

At that moment, I didn't feel like a Super GM. I felt like a mess. I couldn't eat, I couldn't sleep, and even looking at the board felt impossible. I was awake at 3 in the morning, wondering how to pass the time until the late afternoon game. This had been the pattern for several days: winless streaks piling up. First three games without a win, then five, and by the seventh game, I had zero points. My anxiety was through the roof.

To distract myself, I went for a long walk, hit the gym, watched episodes of *Perry Mason* on TV and finally finished breakfast. And then I realized: I still had seven hours to sit with my self-doubt. It felt like the walls of the hotel room were closing in on me.

In moments like this, what you really need is objectivity – the ability to look at things clearly. Without it, a bad tournament can feel worse than it actually is. After a bad move that turns the game against you, the best response is to calm yourself and accept the situation. Thinking that 'I could have won five moves ago' or 'I could have lost three moves ago' doesn't change what's happening now.

It's a bit like a financial investment. If you lose money, staring at what you could have done won't help. What matters is what you still have and what you can do next. One trick I use when things look grim is to imagine I've already lost the point and see how long I can keep my cool. The same goes for winning positions: stay calm, protect your advantage and don't get carried away by early excitement.

One game that taught me this lesson happened at the Intel Chess Grand Prix in 1994 in New York. I was playing Belarusian Israeli GM Ilya Smirin. Both our games in round one had ended in draws, so we went into a tie-break game, an Armageddon blitz decider. Blitz chess is a very fast version of the game, where each player has only a few minutes for the whole match. White got six minutes, Black got five. White had to win, while Black could advance with a draw.

A few moves into a Petroff Defence, Smirin played an unusual move (4.Nxe5). On move 4, I froze. I had already spent over a minute – an eternity in blitz. His move caught me completely off guard. I leaned over the board, almost smelling the pieces, trying to focus.

'C'mon, Vishy, make a move!' the commentators shouted (thankfully, I couldn't hear them clearly). I finally moved my pawn to d6, attacking White's knight and forcing it back. After that, I played quickly, exchanged pieces and slowly wore him down until he made a mistake. My early pause had helped me: I went from hesitating to blitzing through the next 46 moves – and won the game.

That short pause for clarity became a lesson I carried through my career: sometimes stopping to think clearly can change everything.

Back in Dortmund, I wasn't unprepared. But after two defeats – against Topalov and Morozevich – I started playing passively, trying only not to lose. Chess punishes fear. I finished last, with three points out of ten, hitting rock bottom. I told myself: I can't do worse than this.

It was shocking because just months earlier, I had been on one of the best runs of my career: winning the Frankfurt Chess Classic in June, the World Championship in New Delhi and Tehran in December 2000, finishing second at the Corus Tournament in Wijk aan Zee in early 2001 and winning at the Torneo Magistral Ciudad de León in Merida, Mexico, that May. Then came my worst-ever result in Dortmund, followed by losing my World Championship title to Ivanchuk in Moscow that December.

I had to pull myself up. The only way out was the same way I had fallen in – one move at a time.

***

Another thing I've learnt is that you don't always need to rush. Sometimes taking a short pause, even when the game is fast, can make all the difference. It gives your brain a moment to organize ideas, check threats and remember patterns you've studied before. It's like giving your mind a little reboot.

Chess is also a game of patterns. Once you see the design in your opponent's moves, you can predict what might come next. But if you are too stressed or anxious, your mind misses the signals. That's why staying calm is as important as knowing the moves.

Even when I lost repeatedly, I reminded myself to focus on each move separately. I thought: 'Forget the past games. What can I do right now?' By thinking in small steps, I was able to regain some control, even if the scoreboard didn't show it.

Chess, like life, doesn't always go the way you plan. Sometimes you win, sometimes you lose. The important part is to stay calm, learn from mistakes and keep moving forward. Even if you finish last in a tournament, each game teaches you something new.

When I look back, Dortmund was tough, but it reminded me how to handle pressure, disappointment and fear. It reminded me that even Grandmasters are human, and that losing is just part of the journey. The key is to focus on the next move, not the last mistake.

VISHY SAYS

IN CHESS – AND IN LIFE – BAD TIMES WILL COME. WHEN YOU'RE DOWN, DON'T DWELL ON MISTAKES OR WHAT COULD HAVE BEEN. ACCEPT THE MOMENT, PAUSE TO CLEAR YOUR MIND AND FOCUS ON THE NEXT MOVE AHEAD. ONE CALM, CLEAR STEP AT A TIME IS HOW YOU CLIMB BACK UP FROM ROCK BOTTOM. MISTAKES AND LOSSES ARE JUST LESSONS IN DISGUISE.

18

GETTING OVER THE LOWS

The slump I went through didn't happen suddenly. It wasn't as if I woke up one morning in 2001 and started losing every game. In fact, I was still winning enough matches to convince myself that everything was fine. But under the surface, cracks were slowly forming, like tiny leaks in a dam that grew bigger over time. These cracks, unnoticed at first, eventually threatened the whole structure. It's strange how winning can hide problems just as much as losing can reveal them.

This hole I had landed in wasn't completely unexpected. When you keep winning, it's easy to ignore warning signs. You tell yourself that victories prove your approach is perfect. That feeling of success can make you less alert, and you stop checking for weaknesses in your game. Maybe your opening moves aren't as strong as they should be or your strategies are too limited. But as long as you keep winning, you don't notice the alarms. Small flaws slowly turn into big problems. Only when the tide finally turns do you realize you were swimming against the current without noticing.

Seeing this early and being honest with yourself is very important. It lets you trust your instincts and take steps to change before things get worse. For me, this was the turning point that helped me climb out of the slump I faced the year following the turn of the millennium. I decided to skip Wijk aan Zee in 2002, an event I had played every year for a long time, and also the Amber Tournament in Monaco. These were tough decisions, but sometimes stepping back is the only way to move forward.

The breakthrough came at the Dubai Rapid Grand Prix in 2002. The tournament started badly. Faster games should have been my strength, but I was knocked out early in the second round. Normally, that would have been the end of the road. But an unusual rule made it so that players who lost early still had to keep playing for final standings. This turned out to be a blessing. Without the pressure to win to stay in the tournament, I played freely, with nothing to lose. Suddenly, I felt like my younger self – the six-year-old boy who played just for fun. I ended up winning as many games as the eventual winner, Peter Leko.

That experience made me realize something important: my routine needed a shake-up. More good things followed. Before the 2002 Eurotel Trophy in Prague, no one was talking about me as a title contender. That strangely lifted a weight off my shoulders. For the first time in 15 months, Garry Kasparov, Vladimir Kramnik and I were all playing in the same tournament. It was a knockout format with rapid and blitz games, making every match a real test. I battled through the rounds, winning a tense tie-break in the semi-finals against Vassily Ivanchuk, who had just knocked out Kasparov. Then, in the final, I faced Anatoly Karpov. I won the first game as White and drew the second with Black, clinching the title.

Looking back, I believe motivation follows its own rhythm. You can't force it. When it returns, it feels natural, almost effortless. You play your best games not because of pressure, but because you are excited – eager to learn, explore new ideas or just play.

Chess, like many sports, is deeply tied to emotions. If you lose control over your feelings, your play suffers. Opponents often try to shake you, pulling you out of your comfort zone to make you make mistakes. After tough losses, I've felt the sting of self-doubt. Weeks or months later, I would still shudder at a blunder. Two losses against Chinese GM Wang Hao in 2013, for example, haunted me. They made me overthink later games, always expecting failure before it even happened.

This emotional rollercoaster isn't unique to chess. In tennis, smashing your racket after a lost point doesn't fix the problem. In football, missing a last-minute goal can weigh on a team's mind until they get a chance to make up for it. The mind heals best when a bad memory is replaced by a good one – when a new victory overshadows the past defeat.

When things go wrong in chess, it helps to see exactly where you are stuck, make changes and sometimes even change your environment completely. After a tough game, I often go for a run on the treadmill. The physical effort lets me release frustration – it feels like stretching out a raw nerve and making it supple again. When I finish, the loss still stings, but after a shower, a good meal and a night's sleep, I wake up feeling lighter, ready to go again.

If you lose, try this – don't give up next time! But when slumps happen, remember they sneak in quietly and don't leave easily. Still, once you find your way out, you carry that map with you forever.

This map is more than just a chess plan. It's a lesson about life. It's about resilience, patience and courage to face weaknesses instead of ignoring them. Every setback holds the seeds of a comeback if you are willing to learn. The key is not to let success blind you or defeat break you. Stay curious, stay honest with yourself and keep moving forward. Because eventually, even the deepest slump gives way to a new chapter – one where you're stronger, wiser and ready for new challenges. That happens when you learn how to deal with the worst.

VISHY SAYS

SOMETIMES SLUMPS SNEAK UP ON YOU EVEN WHEN YOU'RE STILL WINNING. I LEARNT THAT MOTIVATION CAN'T BE FORCED – IT COMES NATURALLY WHEN YOU ARE CURIOUS AND EXCITED AGAIN. CHESS, LIKE LIFE, IS ABOUT HANDLING EMOTIONS, LEARNING FROM SETBACKS AND MOVING FORWARD ONE STEP AT A TIME.

19

CLIMBING WITHOUT THE LADDER

I lay back on the soft hotel bed in Mexico City, staring up at the ceiling and grinning.

I felt like a World Champion.

And I was.

Usually, after a win, my brain is too busy replaying the moves to let me sleep. But tonight, I wasn't even pretending to try. I just wanted to enjoy the moment.

It was 30 September 2007, and only a few hours earlier I'd been crowned the undisputed World Champion. I was 37 years old. This was actually my second world title – the first had been in Tehran in 2000 – but back then, some people had acted as if it didn't really count. Winning that time had been like running a race, breaking through the ribbon and then hearing someone say, 'Oh wait, you still have a few laps to go.'

The problem had started years earlier, in 1993. Two very influential chess players – Garry Kasparov and English GM Nigel Short – had left FIDE, the main international chess organization, and created their own group. Suddenly, the chess world had two separate championships, two different 'World Champions' and endless debates about who the *real* one was. People took sides and the rivalry was as intense as anything on the chessboard.

Me? I stayed out of it. Picking a side meant making one group happy and the other angry – and honestly, I just wanted to play chess.

By 2007, FIDE had decided to fix things. They organized a single World Championship tournament in Mexico City, bringing together eight of the best players in the world. The winner would get the official title and, the next year, would face Vladimir Kramnik – the previous World Champion – in a one-on-one match in Bonn.

Before the final round, when I was already leading, Kramnik's manager, Carsten Hensel, came to talk to Aruna. The way he described it, it sounded like they thought I'd only be a 'real' champion if I beat Kramnik directly.

Aruna, who was there, didn't flinch. She told him, politely but firmly, that they could play Boris Gelfand (who was behind me) instead if they were in such a hurry. Then came a strange request: I was told that 'under no circumstances' should I speak in German during the match. That made no sense to me. I'd lived in Germany for years, played countless tournaments there and spoke the language fluently. We said no.

The next day, I was standing on the podium in a bright-pink serape, a gold medal around my neck and a laurel wreath on my head. The huge hall was buzzing with cameras clicking, lights flashing and voices in every language. I could see Kramnik in the audience. He didn't clap or smile, but his eyes followed me closely.

He was famous for his rock-solid defence against my favourite first move, 1.e4, especially using the Petroff Defence and the Berlin Variation. I'd played 1.e4 for most of my life, and it felt almost like my signature, the first step of my chess handwriting. But against Kramnik, it was like running into a brick wall again and again.

I was thinking about whether to stick with 1.e4 or try something completely different. Then an idea popped into my head, as suddenly as a light switching on.

'Why don't I open with the 1.d4 against Kramnik?' I said, half to myself.

Standing there on the podium, I told myself I had to cling to this impulse – like climbing an imaginary ladder – and then push the ladder away so I'd have no choice but to keep going up. That's one of the best ways to stop hesitating and make sure you keep moving forward.

The thought both excited and scared me. Switching to 1.d4 meant entering territory that was Kramnik's strength, not mine. He had spent his whole career perfecting those positions, polishing them until they were as sharp as glass. For me, it meant leaving behind the comfort of lines I had played for years. It felt like standing on the edge of a diving board, knowing the water below was deep and full of hidden currents.

When I told Aruna and my coach Peter Heine Nielsen, they exchanged a look, but neither dismissed the idea. Peter simply said, 'We'll have to work very

THE COVER OF *NEW IN CHESS* MAGAZINE, ANNOUNCING MY WORLD CHAMPIONSHIP WIN IN MEXICO CITY IN 2007

hard, but it could surprise him.' That encouragement was enough to keep the thought alive.

The real challenge wouldn't be learning the main lines – it would be mastering all the tiny, tricky positions I didn't yet know. If my plan failed, I might look silly. But the idea of taking this risk gave me energy.

I decided to take full responsibility for the choice. If I got into an unfamiliar position, I'd just have to improvise. Sometimes you do something for the joy of it – for the art, for the sport – rather than to tick off every box in a plan. At least if I ended up in trouble, I'd be in new boring positions rather than the same old boring positions.

Deep down, I knew that if I went through my whole career without taking risks like this, I'd end up hating myself – and maybe even hating chess.

That thought took me back to a day in mid-2006, in the white kitchen of our home in Collado Mediano near Madrid. Frederic Friedel from ChessBase (an online platform for chess software and information) had called to tell me that Kramnik was setting all the terms for the Bonn match. I told Aruna, and we both thought it was unfair that one player had so many privileges and the other guy had none.

'Imagine the plight of that guy,' I had said then. 'The good thing is I don't need to worry about it right now. It's not my problem until I win.' I decided to focus on winning Mexico first, a practical step, rather than deal with hypothetical scenarios.

Turns out, it *was* my problem.

But a *good* problem, haha.

VISHY SAYS

SOMETIMES YOU MAY WIN A PRIZE, FINISH A RACE OR ACHIEVE A GOAL, AND YET PEOPLE SAY IT DOESN'T COUNT UNTIL YOU'VE DONE MORE. THAT CAN FEEL UNFAIR. AND FRUSTRATING. YOU CAN SPEND ALL YOUR TIME TRYING TO PROVE THEM WRONG, OR YOU CAN FOCUS ON WHAT YOU LOVE DOING, AND KEEP GOING. IF YOU STAY CALM AND FOCUSED, YOUR RESULTS WILL SPEAK LOUDER THAN ANY DEBATE. AND SOMETIMES WHEN YOU'RE FACED WITH A WALL, THE ONLY WAY FORWARD IS TO LEAP OVER IT.

20

A LEAP OF FAITH

The day after the closing ceremony in Mexico City, I woke up with the strange feeling of having achieved something I'd dreamt of for years but also sensing that the real challenge was still ahead. I was the World Champion now, officially and undisputedly. Yet even as I celebrated, I knew what was coming next: I would have to defend my title in a one-on-one match against Vladimir Kramnik.

That thought stayed with me as I packed my bags: 'Why don't I open with 1.d4 against Kramnik?'

The more I thought about it, the more it felt like standing at the base of a tall ladder. If I climbed carefully, rung by rung, I could always come back down to safety. But if someone suddenly pulled the ladder away, there would be no turning back – I would have to leap upward and hope I could keep going. Switching from 1.e4 to 1.d4 against Kramnik would be exactly like that: a leap of faith.

Of course, deep down, I knew what I was setting myself up for. Kramnik had been playing 1.d4 all his life, and he knew every response, every subtle twist of the opening. I would be walking into his turf, like stepping onto a battlefield he had already prepared. But I also knew something else: if I stuck to 1.e4, I'd be predictable, and at the highest level, predictability is dangerous.

***

The build-up to Bonn in 2008 was intense. Kramnik's manager had already made it clear that some people wouldn't see me as a 'real' World Champion until I beat Kramnik directly. The comments didn't anger me, but they gave me extra motivation. If I lost the match, nobody would care if my arguments were clever or not: that it was not fair in format or legal terms. . .or whatever. If I won this match, there would be no morc debates.

We spent months preparing. My team of seconds and I worked through countless d4 lines, and I knew I was still a little less experienced than Kramnik in this territory. But I kept telling myself: if I take this risk, it will be for the joy of the game, for the art and the challenge, not just to tick boxes in a plan.

Finally, the match began. In the first game, I played 1.d4. It was like stepping into cold water – shocking at first but strangely refreshing. Kramnik hadn't expected it and that gave me a small psychological edge. He settled into his usual solid play, but I could see from the way he adjusted in his chair that he was just a little uncomfortable.

By the third game, I managed to break through. I scored my first win with Black, and the victory gave me confidence that this was worth it. In the fifth game, I struck again, and by the time we reached the halfway point, I was leading the match. Each time I sat at the board, I reminded myself that I was no longer climbing carefully rung by rung – I had pushed away the ladder, and there was no going back.

The most memorable game came in round 6. Again, I opened with 1.d4. Kramnik miscalculated in a critical moment. I pounced with precise moves and, suddenly, the board lit up with possibilities. When the final blow landed and Kramnik realized he was lost, he leaned back with a stunned expression. That game became one of the highlights of my career.

From that point on, the momentum was mine. I didn't need to take unnecessary risks; I simply had to play solidly and not allow Kramnik back into the match. By the twelfth and final game, the result was clear: I had won 6½–4½, defending my new title and proving once and for all that I was the true World Champion.

Standing on the stage in Bonn, hearing the applause, I thought back to that spark of an idea in Mexico City: 'Why don't I play 1.d4 against Kramnik?' It had felt risky, almost reckless, but it had changed everything. Without that leap of faith, I might have been trapped in the same old battles, playing predictably and giving Kramnik the upper hand.

Instead, I had reinvented myself at just the right time.

VISHY SAYS

WHEN A BIG CHALLENGE COMES, YOU DON'T ALWAYS HAVE TO TAKE THE SAFE ROUTE. IF YOU BELIEVE IN A DIFFERENT PATH, STICK TO IT. IN CHESS, AS IN LIFE, THE BOLDEST MOVES OFTEN LEAD TO THE MOST REWARDING VICTORIES.

SOMETIMES IN LIFE, THE SAFEST PATH ISN'T REALLY SAFE AT ALL – IT JUST LOCKS YOU INTO THE SAME OLD PATTERNS. TAKING A LEAP OF FAITH DOESN'T MEAN BEING RECKLESS; IT MEANS TRUSTING YOURSELF ENOUGH TO TRY SOMETHING NEW, EVEN IF IT FEELS RISKY.

21

COOL AS ICE

Some players panic when things go wrong. Others… play cards all night.

In Seville in 1987, Kasparov found himself down 11–12 in his World Championship match against Karpov. You might expect him to spend that long night hunched over chess books and analysis, desperately trying to solve every problem on the board before the next game. But instead, he did something surprising. He sat at a table with his team, shuffling decks of cards, dealing hands and playing card games late into the night.

Kasparov knew something important: when your mind is a tangled mess of nerves and anxiety, clear thinking becomes impossible. No sudden lightning-bolt solution is going to strike in the middle of a sleepless night. Sometimes the smartest move is to step away, give your mind a chance to rest and be ready to pick up the fight freshly the next day.

He understood that panicking doesn't help. In fact, it can make things worse. Often, giving yourself time to recover and calm down is more valuable than any flash of inspiration born from stress. No matter how well you prepare, if your emotions are rattled, you probably won't be able to use all your preparation effectively.

On the day of the next match game, Kasparov woke up in the afternoon, had a leisurely lunch and told himself to just 'keep things going'. His plan wasn't to dazzle with fireworks but to keep enough pieces on the board and play solid, reliable chess. His team hadn't analysed every possible variation, but they had solid starting points ready for each line. That way, Kasparov could improvise, add a bit of creativity and respond flexibly depending on how the game unfolded.

I've often used that same approach in my own career. Sometimes I decide to experiment with one part of my opening repertoire and keep the other parts solid. The aim isn't to cover every possible move my opponent might make – that's impossible – but to prepare loosely for the eight or nine most likely possibilities. This strategy leaves less room for nasty surprises and keeps me mentally agile.

Take my 1998 World Championship match against Karpov in Lausanne. He was obviously satisfied with a draw. I decided to follow Kasparov's strategy and pulled out an unusual opening: the Trompowsky. It's an aggressive, tricky system that often leads to strange and unfamiliar positions early on. The move caught Karpov off guard, and in his discomfort, he gave me a rare opportunity that gave me an edge in the match.

No matter how you feel inside, being hard to read at the board is a skill worth mastering.

I don't usually show my emotions openly, but opponents who know me well can sometimes spot tiny

PLAYING KARPOV AT THE FIDE WORLD CHAMPIONSHIP IN LAUSANNE IN 1998

giveaways – a shift in my posture, a certain look in my eyes – that hint at panic, joy or frustration. Some players like to bluff by acting overconfident or pretending to be angry with themselves. It's all part of the mental game.

I tend to prefer staying quiet, calm, and revealing as little as possible. I want to keep my opponents guessing. My one real weakness? Nail-biting. If I've blundered or sense trouble ahead, my nails disappear fast. It's a visible cue, so I've tried hard to control it, but it's still an instinct I struggle to hide.

***

Other players have their own ways of handling emotions at the board. Vladimir Kramnik, for example, sometimes launches sudden attacks when he's in trouble, trying to make it seem like everything is part of his plan. Kasparov is known for his dramatic scowl and fierce glares – masterful acting that works because he's such a strong player that his opponents take him seriously. Magnus Carlsen, on the other hand, is famously hard to read. He can look relaxed and confident at the same time, giving nothing away.

I remember at the 2019 Grand Chess Tour in Croatia, I played the move Ke3 against Carlsen. It improved my position, but I couldn't tell if he'd spotted the danger. I watched his face for clues, but he gave away nothing. Then he spent a long 25 minutes thinking – far longer than usual at that stage. That's when I realized I'd caught him by surprise. The game eventually ended in a draw, but that moment confirmed the power of staying cool and unreadable.

Sometimes you can sense a blunder coming a few moves ahead. It's a strange intuition, probably born from being deeply tuned in to the board and your opponent's style. One subtle clue I often watch for is breathing patterns. Even when a player keeps a calm face, a wavering or held breath can give them away. When an opponent suddenly stops breathing for a moment, I know there's something on the board worth hunting for. More often than not, that's exactly where I find my chance.

The mental battle in chess goes beyond the moves on the board. How you handle yourself when the pressure rises, how well you can read the person across from you, can decide the game before a single piece moves.

Keeping your cool is a skill you learn with experience. It's about staying calm when the world feels like it's spinning out of control, about hiding your emotions so your opponent can't use them against you and about watching every twitch or breath for the tiniest hint of weakness.

Because in chess, the moment your opponent gives away a clue, the game might be yours. But it's always a fight for sure.

VISHY SAYS

WHEN THINGS GET TOUGH, PANICKING ONLY MAKES IT HARDER TO THINK CLEARLY. SOMETIMES THE SMART CHOICE IS TO TAKE A BREAK, RELAX YOUR MIND AND COME BACK FRESH. STAYING CALM AND COMPOSED HELPS YOU STAY IN CONTROL AND KEEPS OTHERS GUESSING ABOUT YOUR NEXT MOVE. PAY ATTENTION TO SMALL SIGNS THAT REVEAL WHAT OTHERS MIGHT BE FEELING OR PLANNING.

MASTERING YOUR EMOTIONS IS JUST AS IMPORTANT AS MASTERING SKILLS – BECAUSE SUCCESS OFTEN DEPENDS ON MENTAL STRENGTH AS MUCH AS ON TECHNIQUE.

22

ON BALANCE

Generally, my parents kept me grounded. You know, the attitude about not tempting the gods, and keeping a straight head on one's shoulders, and not getting cocky. I would repress any overconfidence, even while feeling that I was not going to lose. Overconfidence can often sabotage effort – or at least later you may feel that you didn't win because you had let down your guard.

The best way to go forward is with confidence, but not with the feeling that you are infallible. The world can be quite random and some things are beyond one's control. The best approach is to move ahead with a healthy humility and with the understanding that you cannot control all factors.

REAL INNER STRENGTH COMES FROM BEING CONFIDENT BUT ALSO FROM BEING HUMBLE.

VISHY SAYS

23

NICE GUYS FINISH... PRETTY WELL

Sports can be tough. You play to win, and to win, you have to beat your opponent. That often means facing conflict – sometimes on the board, sometimes off it. And confrontation isn't something I'm naturally comfortable with. I prefer to avoid head-on clashes whenever possible. But looking back, I realize there have been times when I probably should have been more assertive, even if it felt uncomfortable.

Take the Dortmund tournament in 1997. My opponent, Anatoly Karpov, arrived 40 minutes late for our game. Whether it was intentional or just carelessness, it felt like he was trying to unsettle me. By five minutes past the official start, it was clear the arbiter wouldn't step in unless I made a fuss. Karpov explained his taxi was delayed, but I didn't fully believe him. I faced a choice: complain and risk tension, or let it go and focus on the game. I chose the latter, saving my energy for the match ahead.

PLAYING IN DORTMUND, 1996

Others might handle this differently. Vladimir Kramnik always made his annoyance very clear when something felt unfair. Garry Kasparov and Magnus Carlsen likely wouldn't have accepted such treatment. I admire that boldness – the ability to face conflict straight on. I also saw it in Nieves, my proxy parent who always helped me and fought in my corner to solve problems, from hotel bookings to visas.

But being confrontational isn't just one bold moment. It's a continuous process – clarifying your position, standing firm and sometimes living with tension. I don't thrive in that kind of environment. My best chess comes when I'm happy, calm and focused, not distracted by battles off the board. Maybe that's why I sometimes seem like a pushover – tidy shirts, neat hair, friendly manner – but I'm okay with that.

I'm reminded of Zinedine Zidane head-butting Marco Materazzi in the 2006 FIFA World Cup final. Many were shocked, but I understood it in context – raw emotion in response to something deeply personal. I often think about standing up to bad behaviour, but I don't feel comfortable with hostility or retaliation. My philosophy is simple: let your performance speak. Complaining only makes you sound like a whiner. Instead, I focus on the next game.

***

Sometimes the toughest challenges come off the board. I remember the Norway Chess tournament in Stavanger in June 2015. It came just after one of the most painful moments of my life – the passing of my mother. I share this with you, though you are young, because grief is part of life and learning to cope is important. On the night of 26 May, I got a call from my father at 1:18 a.m. My mother wasn't waking up. I called an ambulance and raced to their home. She had passed quietly in her sleep hours earlier.

Nothing in chess had prepared me for that shock. Amma had been my chess partner, early coach, loudest cheerleader, travel companion, guide, agent and protector for decades, besides being Mum, of course. The days that followed were a blur. I stayed surrounded by family and friends, and kept my mind busy with conversations. The rituals of mourning ended just before my flight to Norway.

On the plane, reality hit me fully. I cried, overwhelmed with guilt for things left unsaid. In Stavanger, far from home, I cried every day. I channelled my grief into my games. Somehow, despite it all, I played some of the best chess of my life, finishing second, just half a point behind the winner, Veselin Topalov. By the end, I felt a little stronger, a little healed.

When I'm angry, sad or frustrated, I have a simple therapy: walking. I can walk for hours without noticing where I'm going. I love walking in forested areas. The real purpose is to let bottled-up emotions spill out safely. If feelings stay trapped, they burst at the worst moments, clouding judgment and causing mistakes. Strong emotions can get in the way of learning and clear thinking. I train myself to pause during critical moments, organize my thoughts and act calmly.

I remember the Dortmund tournament in 2003. I'd just lost two games in a row – to Azerbaijani GM Teimour Radjabov and Moldovan GM Victor Bologan. Furious with myself, I stormed outside for a walk. Aruna followed silently. 'Have nothing to say?' I snapped at her. She waited until I asked again. Then softly, she said, 'Tomorrow will be better. Maybe you should try breathing deeply.' That was some of the best advice I've ever received.

Tomorrow is likely to be better – if you prepare yourself to meet it.

VISHY SAYS

SOMETIMES YOU HAVE TO STAND UP FOR YOURSELF, EVEN IF IT FEELS SCARY. BUT YOU DON'T ALWAYS NEED TO SHOUT OR ARGUE. IT'S BETTER TO STAY CALM AND FOCUS ON WHAT REALLY MATTERS.

WHEN YOU FEEL UPSET OR ANGRY, TAKE DEEP BREATHS OR GO FOR A WALK. BEING STRONG MEANS STAYING CALM, LEARNING FROM MISTAKES AND TRYING AGAIN TOMORROW WITH A FRESH MIND AND HEART.

24

HOW TO PREPARE (WITHOUT FEELING LIKE IT'S HOMEWORK)

If you've ever had a parent or teacher lecture you about preparation, you've probably rolled your eyes and muttered, 'Here we go again.' They always say: study, review, revise…and then revise again. It can feel boring, like homework you don't want to do. But actually, they're right.

I learnt this lesson early in my chess career and kept it with me throughout. Preparation doesn't just happen the night before a match; it starts weeks or even months ahead – like planting seeds that you harvest much later. Chess, like many things, rewards patience and steady effort more than sudden bursts.

In 1998, I spoke with Ken Thompson, one of the inventors of UNIX and the B programming language, the basis for much of modern computing. At the time, computers were already better at short-term calculations, but humans still had an edge in long-term strategy. When I asked if machines would ever catch up, he said, 'Of course! Strategy is just long-term tactics.'

That idea stuck with me. Over time, I saw how true it was. Chess is mostly tactics. If your tactics fail, even the best strategy can't save you. Strategy without careful moves falls apart at the first problem. But if you play well, you can manage even without a perfect plan.

For me, planning a game isn't about arranging some magical set of moves. It's about thinking what my opponent might want, knowing my own goals and steering the game toward them. Strategy is a tricky word – hard to define and harder to apply – but you need a framework where every detail fits together.

Most of that work happens long before the first move. Unlike sports where coaches shout from the sidelines, chess players have an invisible team working behind the scenes. They review openings, prepare surprises and study opponents' habits.

I remember my first real team during my Candidates match against Russian GM Alexey Dreev in 1991. (Candidates tournaments are where top players compete to decide who will challenge the World Champion.) I had Ferdinand Hellers, a self-taught but methodical friend from the junior circuit, and John van der Wiel from the Netherlands, full of practical experience. Their guidance made my work more efficient and realistic.

When I learnt that I would face Karpov in the Candidates quarter-finals in Brussels, I needed someone who understood him well. A friend recommended Mikhail Gurevich, who had worked with Kasparov. Gurevich's

THE CANDIDATES MATCH I WON AGAINST ALEXEY DREEV IN 1991
PAVED THE WAY FOR MORE WINS TO COME

discipline was impressive – he even confiscated my Walkman to keep me focused (that was more annoying than impressive at first!). We studied Karpov's games, learnt how he pressured opponents and practised blocking his plans. It was exhausting but effective.

In the early 1990s, I met Elizbar Ubilava, who also worked with Karpov. In 1994, we formalized our partnership. Ubilava's creativity pushed me beyond dogmatic training and made my thinking more flexible. He shared stories showing even champions had weaknesses. By the time we parted ways in the early 2000s, my preparation methods had advanced greatly.

Another source of learning was studying past masters. In 2001, I turned to the pioneers and world champions of the 1920s, 30s and 40s: Alexander Alekhine, Emmanuel Lasker and José Raúl Capablanca. Their games, some nearly a hundred years old, felt surprisingly modern. Alekhine, before his 1927 World Championship match with Capablanca, studied his opponent's strengths and weaknesses carefully. Mikhail Botvinnik was the first world-class chess player from within the Soviet Union – his 1961 rematch with Tal showed how preparation can help you handle chaos calmly. From both, I learnt that studying an opponent isn't about copying moves. You must feel the pressure they felt and imagine the board as they saw it.

VISHY SAYS

PREPARATION ISN'T JUST ABOUT KNOWING OTHERS – IT'S ABOUT KNOWING YOURSELF. THE BEST PREPARATION SHARPENS WHO YOU ALREADY ARE.

UNDERSTANDING YOUR STRENGTHS, WEAKNESSES, COMFORT ZONES AND BLIND SPOTS IS THE REAL KEY. WHEN YOU PREPARE, TRY TO UNDERSTAND NOT ONLY WHAT OTHERS MIGHT DO, BUT ALSO WHAT *YOU* DO BEST. THAT'S WHERE TRUE PROGRESS BEGINS. BY KNOWING YOURSELF!

25

GETTING TO KNOW YOURSELF

In chess, theory never stands still. Every month, there's a new line in an opening, a computer-suggested move or a trendy gambit that sweeps through tournaments. But the goal stays the same: upset the usual order, pull your opponent out of their comfort zone and get them into the kind of fight you want. How you do this depends a lot on the kind of player you are.

Broadly, there are two types. A 'horizontal' player spreads out like a wide tree, a banyan – flexible, adaptable, ready to respond to anything the opponent does. The 'banyans' can switch systems, change plans midway and leave the other player wondering, 'Where will they go next?' Catching a horizontal player in a trap is tricky because they rarely stay in one place.

A 'vertical' player focuses straight ahead, digging deeply into one opening or plan, like a tall, straight tree, a palm. The 'palms' explore it obsessively, minutely, learning every small detail that could change the game.

You can often guess where a vertical player will fight, but their preparation there can be very strong.

Each style has its pros and cons. A horizontal player might never go deep enough to dominate in one area. A vertical player can become predictable and vulnerable if someone pushes the game outside their chosen track. Most players naturally lean toward one style, but trying both is helpful. The horizontal approach teaches flexibility; the vertical approach teaches depth. The ideal balance is rare and hard to maintain.

Some players can switch between the two depending on the situation. I've done this myself – going narrow and focused on a match against someone I know well, and broad and adaptable in a tournament with many different players. Modern chess requires this flexibility. One day you face a teenage prodigy with the latest computer analysis; the next, a veteran who has seen it all before.

A good method is to prepare broadly at first – study many openings and types of positions – then narrow your focus closer to the game. Maybe you reduce your preparation to five main options, then two likely scenarios. Against someone who thrives on surprises, you might keep preparation lighter but wider, ready to improvise. The key question is always: what gives me the best chance to win – going deep or going broad?

That's where curiosity comes in. Without it, you won't explore openings you don't usually play, and you'll miss chances to surprise your opponent. The best players I've met are also the most curious. They ask, 'What if

I try this system? How does this position feel from the other side? Why do so many players avoid this move?'

Curiosity widens your toolkit, sharpens your instincts and makes you more agile. It lets you spot a hidden resource at exactly the right moment. Players who learn flexibility early gain a huge advantage later, especially when opponents target their favourite lines. If you can't change direction mid-game, you will eventually get stuck.

It's the same outside chess. If your main skill is replaced by a machine or given to someone else, and you have no other skills, adapting is hard. Twenty years ago, a purely vertical chess player could survive. Today, that's impossible. Everyone has access to the same databases, computers and opening knowledge. Variety is what sets you apart.

Curiosity also helps with positions you dislike. I've always found quiet positions frustrating – when the board looks even and nothing seems to happen. Magnus Carlsen, however, uses these positions like a craftsman uses a chisel. In the 2013 World Championship, he took a quiet position against me and, move by move, squeezed tiny advantages until I cracked. It was maddening – and impressive.

To get better at positions you dislike, ask yourself: 'What goes wrong here? Do I lose focus? Run out of ideas?' Even a 'boring' position can become a challenge if you set a goal: 'Let me handle this endgame well', or 'Let me keep this equal position equal'. If the same problem shows up in practice games as in real tournaments, you've found a weakness to work on.

The deeper you go into preparation, the more confident you feel at the board. Your goal is to win, and everything from openings to middle-game calculation to endgame technique matters.

When I calculate a long, complicated line, I always check it carefully afterward. The longer the line, the greater the chance of a hidden mistake. Sometimes, in the excitement of a brilliant idea, I overlook something simple. My error-checking is separate from moving the pieces. I ask: 'What did I miss in similar positions? What do other players often overlook here? Which past games are like this? Are there habits that might cause mistakes?'

Often, a game turns when a piece you forgot about – a pawn far away or a knight sitting quietly – suddenly becomes important. There's a kind of justice when the unnoticed piece ends up saving the game.

I remember the 1993 PCA qualifiers in Groningen in the Netherlands against Alexander Beliavsky, a chess player who played for the Soviet Union, Ukraine and Slovenia at different times. I had to choose between a clever sideline to avoid his preparation or the main line. Usually, I avoided the main line, worried about hidden surprises. That day, I boldly went into the main line. It worked – I found an idea that gave him serious problems, and I won.

That success wasn't just luck. It happened because I faced the challenge, trusted my curiosity and took the leap. In life too, an underused skill or overlooked strength can be the resource that gets you through a difficult situation.

The heart of it all is knowing yourself – understanding the resources you have, even if you're not using them today. Sometimes they're buried deep, waiting for the right moment. When that moment comes, you must be ready to use them. That's when preparation, curiosity and adaptability meet – and that's when you give yourself the best chance to win.

VISHY SAYS

PREPARING FOR SOMETHING IMPORTANT ISN'T LAST-MINUTE STUDYING – IT'S LIKE PLANTING SEEDS THAT GROW OVER TIME. IT TAKES PATIENCE AND STEADY EFFORT. PRACTISE YOUR OWN STRENGTHS AND LEARN FROM YOUR MISTAKES.

PREPARATION HELPS YOU FEEL READY AND CONFIDENT, SO YOU DON'T HAVE TO WORRY AT THE LAST MINUTE. REMEMBER, GETTING READY ISN'T BORING HOMEWORK – IT'S HOW YOU GIVE YOURSELF THE BEST CHANCE TO DO YOUR BEST!

26

TAKING RISKS

Have you ever stood at the edge of a diving board, heart racing, wondering whether to jump? Or raised your hand in class to answer a tough question, not fully sure if you were right? That mix of excitement and nervousness is exactly what taking a risk feels like.

In chess, that moment comes when you can either play it safe or make a move that could completely change the game. Sometimes that leap works brilliantly. Other times…not so much. But every risk, whether you win or lose, teaches you something for next time.

Some situations call for risks you aren't completely certain about. I've had both kinds of experiences – times when I made a move at the last minute and it worked perfectly, and others when I tried something I didn't know well and it ended badly.

The best approach is to have a little surprise ready. You may know part of the idea, understand roughly what your opponent might do, and decide to take the risk – but you must accept that you may not know every detail. Naturally, this shouldn't be completely random, like going into a position you know nothing about.

You want to surprise your opponent but not end up surprising yourself.

That means you need a starting point – some preparation already done so that when you improvise at the board, you're not starting from zero. Even a little preparation improves your chances.

And of course, I've been on the other side of surprises too.

One famous example came in my 1995 World Championship match against Garry Kasparov, when he used the Dragon against me. No, not a fire-breathing one – the Dragon is a sharp, aggressive opening in the Sicilian Defence. I hadn't expected it at all. In game 11, it caught me completely off guard, and I lost. He tried it again in game 13 and, even though I knew more about it, I still made big mistakes. Suddenly, the Dragon – which I could have handled – seemed brilliant.

That's the power of surprise: it can shake you so much that even when you know the danger, it's hard to steady yourself.

Risk-taking in chess isn't always about attacking. Sometimes even the threat of an attack is more effective than the real thing. I often held a move in reserve until the right moment. Hinting at danger – like a possible kingside attack – can unsettle your opponent. It's often harder to deal with a vague threat than a direct one, because people start worrying about what might happen.

But there's a balance. Trying to be perfect in chess – going deep until you know a move inside out – is useful, but it can become a problem against some players. You need to judge when their move is strong

NEW YORK, 1995 – THE MATCH THAT TAUGHT ME A GREAT MANY LESSONS

and when it's a bluff. Sometimes you must trust your gut that the 'perfect move' isn't worth chasing if it risks a bigger mistake.

This idea goes beyond chess. Trying for perfection is good for learning, but when you have a deadline or an unpredictable situation, it can hold you back. Part of you may want to get every detail right, but another part – the voice of reason in your head – knows you don't have the time or resources to do that right now.

In those cases, I find short bursts of focused work as effective as long sessions. When you give your full attention to a problem for a short time, you often achieve more. If you work too long, your mind drifts, energy drops and effort is wasted.

Short bursts are like mini sprints – you go all in, then take a break. The best concentration comes from working on something that genuinely interests you. If the task is boring, setting small goals helps you push through.

In a chess game, focus is crucial, but it's also important to take small breaks. If you have time on the clock, let your mind wander a bit, then snap back before making your move.

Sometimes, when I'm in a tricky position, I think about something completely unrelated – a scene from *Monty Python's Holy Grail* or a funny moment from the British political sitcom *Yes Minister* (look it up!). You can pick your own escape. It lightens your mood and gives space to breathe. If it's my opponent's turn, I might walk around instead of obsessing over every possible move.

Sometimes, very odd things pop into my head. During a tie-break game at the 2012 World Championship against Boris Gelfand, I had my son Akhil's nursery rhyme 'Pat a Cake' looping in my mind. Not exactly Grandmaster-level music, but it helped me relax.

In the end, taking risks isn't about being careless – it's about being brave enough to try something new when there are no guarantees. Sometimes you'll

WEARING A LAUREL WREATH IS TRULY EPIC: AFTER MY WIN AT THE WORLD CHAMPIONSHIP IN 2012 IN MOSCOW

succeed, sometimes you will fail, but every time you learn something about your game and yourself.

So, the next time you're standing on your own 'diving board' – whether across the chessboard or in real life – take a deep breath, trust what you know and take the leap. It might be the move that changes everything.

The thing about risks is that they work best when you have a strong base to fall back on. You can leap higher if you know there's solid ground beneath you. In chess – and in life – that 'solid ground' is built from the habits you repeat every day, the things you do without thinking.

That's where routine comes in.

VISHY SAYS

TAKING RISKS CAN FEEL SCARY – LIKE STANDING ON A DIVING BOARD, NOT SURE IF YOU'LL JUMP. SOMETIMES, IN GAMES OR IN LIFE, YOU HAVE TO TRY SOMETHING NEW EVEN IF YOU'RE NOT 100 PER CENT SURE IT WILL WORK. THE KEY IS TO PREPARE FIRST, SO YOU HAVE A STRONG BASE TO SUPPORT YOU. IT'S OKAY IF YOU DON'T GET IT RIGHT EVERY TIME BECAUSE EACH RISK HELPS YOU LEARN AND GROW. SO, WHEN YOU FACE A CHALLENGE, BE BRAVE, HAVE FAITH IN WHAT YOU KNOW AND LEAP OFF!

27

LOOKING UP TO SOMEONE

Over the years, I have drawn inspiration from many people. Some were great historical figures who lived by strong values and moral codes, like Gandhi, who went to extraordinary lengths to avoid violence. As you grow older, though, you come to see that every person has many sides, and it isn't always possible to admire someone completely. Even so, you can choose from the lessons they leave behind to help you in the choices you make.

I've often found myself copying qualities I admired – sometimes without even realizing it. Even my chess rivals, like Kasparov and Kramnik, influenced me; there were things they did better than I did, and I learnt from them. Beyond chess, I have admired tennis players, footballers, actors – especially those who carried themselves with dignity in public. Inspiration has also come from quieter figures: friends of my parents, people who showed dedication to their work and those who refused to give up after setbacks. Their example showed me that focus and perseverance are just as important as skill.

When you're young, it feels natural to look up to many people, be a 'fan' and treat them as heroes. Later, you understand that no one is flawless – but that does not erase the value of the lessons they gave you. Their determination, courage and integrity are qualities worth carrying forward.

WE DON'T NEED PERFECT HEROES – ONLY THE READINESS TO LEARN FROM THE BEST QUALITIES IN OTHERS.

VISHY SAYS

28

ROUTINE – BORING? NO, SCORING!

Have you ever noticed how some days feel like they flow – you wake up, things happen in the right order and you're in control – while on others you're scrambling to find your socks five minutes before leaving the house? A lot of that difference comes down to routine: what you do, when you do it and how consistently you repeat it.

It might sound dull at first. Who wants to do the same thing every day? Where's the adventure in that? But here's the thing – routine is a secret weapon. It keeps your mind clear, your body ready and your focus sharp. Whether you're getting ready for school, a music performance, a football game or a big chess match, a routine means you're not wasting energy on little, unimportant decisions. You have more mental power left for the big ones – the moves that matter.

Routine may not be the most glamorous part of preparation, but it's one of the most important. Sticking to one is about discipline, yes, but also about removing friction from your day. You're creating an environment where good performance becomes easier. Steve Jobs wore the same black turtleneck every day, Mark Zuckerberg sticks to a grey T-shirt. Why? Because one less decision in the morning frees their mind for the decisions that count.

For me, the chess equivalent of a tennis player fussing over their racquet grip or a cricketer knocking in a new bat is arriving in the tournament city a couple of days early. I like to walk around its streets, look for interesting food joints, maybe even try them out. None of this is part of 'official chess preparation', but it's part of my mental settling-in process. I'm reducing the 'unknowns' before the first game. By the time I sit down at the board, the place already feels familiar.

Some parts of my routine aren't strategic at all – they just snuck in over time and stayed. My match shirts, for instance. I'm not overly fussy, but a few have developed an unshakeable reputation for bringing good results. There's a particular black shirt with red stripes and a white collar that could probably be inducted into my personal Hall of Fame. I wore it when I beat Levon Aronian and Veselin Topalov, and drew Sergey Karjakin to qualify at the 2014 Candidates in Khanty-Mansiysk in Russia. I wore it during my win against Aronian at Wijk aan Zee in 2013 – one of my best games ever – and during a string of successes in 2007.

Of course, I've also lost while wearing that shirt – but somehow the brain files those results in a separate folder marked 'Ignore'. It's easier, and more pleasant, to remember the wins and think, 'This is my luckiest

BEAMING AFTER WINNING THE RAPID SECTION OF THE 11TH TAL MEMORIAL IN 2018 IN MOSCOW

shirt.' In Riyadh, at the 2017 World Rapid & Blitz, I finally decided to let go of the superstition. My results weren't magically improving because of what I wore. If they had been, I might have invested in a dozen identical shirts and saved myself a lot of opening preparation.

It's not just shirts. Certain pens I've used for match notes make repeat appearances. At times, I've even had separate 'black pen' and 'white pen' systems, depending on which colour pieces I'm playing. I've convinced myself that skipping my usual omelette before a game could cost me a point or that eating something unfamiliar might jinx my luck. Deep down, I know it's silly to believe that the thickness of my pen line or the number of egg yolks in my breakfast can influence the result on the board. But before an important game, the mind is like a child clutching a favourite blanket – it searches for familiar patterns that feel safe.

The flip side of routine is what happens when you don't have one. At rapid and blitz events in Berlin (2015) and Doha (2016), my results were well below what I expected of myself. The pairings were slow to be announced, the playing hall was crowded, and between games I drifted aimlessly. Without anything constructive to occupy my time, my focus leaked away, bit by bit. My mind felt like a kite without a string – it was moving, but not in the right direction.

In Riyadh in 2017, I decided to change that. I carried my laptop, solved chess puzzles between rounds and even watched short videos just to keep my mind engaged. I created a mini routine for the gaps between games, so I never felt adrift. It worked – I won the rapid title that year.

That's the other truth about routine: it's not about doing the *same* thing everywhere. It's about creating the right *conditions* to think clearly and feel confident, even if those conditions look different depending on where you are.

And sometimes routine becomes a safety net when you need it most. Chess tournaments can be mentally brutal – you can feel on top of the world after one round, and crushed the next. In those moments, falling back on familiar habits gives you a foothold. Eat the same breakfast, go for the same walk, review your openings in the same order: it doesn't guarantee a win, but it gives you something steady to hold on to while the rest of the tournament feels like a storm.

Of course, you also need the flexibility to break your own routine when it's no longer serving you. If your 'lucky' shirt is actually making you overheat in the hall, ditch it. If your usual breakfast leaves you sluggish in a new time zone, change it. Routine should be a tool to help you, not a trap.

***

Over the years, I've learnt that the best routines are the ones you build consciously. They should be shaped around your actual needs, not just inherited from your past or copied from someone else. A routine that works for me might frustrate you; what works for you might feel unnatural to me. But the core principles remain: remove small decisions, create familiarity, save energy for the moments that matter.

When you look at it that way, routine is really about self-knowledge. It forces you to notice what helps you focus, what distracts you, what calms you down and what throws you off. And that's where it links to something much bigger – because preparation, self-knowledge and habits are the base layer of performance in anything. The real challenge is what you *build* on that base.

A solid routine can make you sharper, calmer and more resilient. But it's only the starting point. In chess, as in life, you still have to use your skills, adapt to surprises and take calculated risks. The opening ritual gets you to the board in good shape. What happens after that is up to your moves – both the literal ones on the chessboard, and the choices you make off it.

So yes – routine may look boring from the outside. But inside, it's quietly doing its job, saving you from a hundred tiny distractions, making sure your energy goes where it matters most. And when the moment comes – when the pressure is on and you need to play your best – you might find that your 'boring' routine was really your secret weapon all along.

VISHY SAYS

ROUTINE MIGHT SOUND BORING, BUT IT'S ACTUALLY A SUPERPOWER! WHEN YOU DO CERTAIN THINGS THE SAME WAY EVERY DAY, YOU SAVE YOUR BRAIN EXTRA WORK. THIS HELPS YOU STAY CALM AND FOCUSED FOR THE IMPORTANT STUFF. ROUTINES MAKE YOUR DAY RUN SMOOTHLY AND GIVE YOU A STEADY FEELING, ESPECIALLY WHEN THINGS GET TRICKY. AND THE BEST ROUTINES ARE ONES YOU CREATE YOURSELF, TO HELP YOU FEEL READY AND CONFIDENT.

29

THE MAKING OF A CHAMPION

Have you ever practised really hard for something – like a big match, a tough exam or a school play – and still felt like things didn't go the way you hoped? That's how it felt for me during my first World Championship match. I was 25 years old, full of hope, and ready to play the best chess of my life. But what I didn't realize was how different – and how difficult – a World Championship match could be.

Let me take you back to New York City, to a chessboard set up on the 107th floor of the World Trade Center. Yes, you read that right – we were playing chess more than 1,300 feet in the air! From the windows, we could see all of Manhattan, the rivers and tiny yellow taxis below. But I wasn't there to admire the view. I was there to face Garry Kasparov, the strongest chess player in the world.

Kasparov was already a five-time World Champion. His reputation was huge. He played fast, sharp chess. He had books, fans and a full support team helping him with every detail. Me? I had my experience from tournaments, my training camp in Madrid and my own love for the game.

I had worked very hard to get there. I had played many tournaments to qualify, spent months training, and gone through a lot of ups and downs. I even held a training camp in my house in Madrid, with four strong seconds helping me. We studied positions, tried different openings and prepared for Kasparov's favourite lines. At the end of each day, my brain felt like a sponge – soaked and squeezed dry.

But even before the first pawn was moved, surprises were underway.

Originally, the match was supposed to be in Cologne, Germany. So, I booked hotel rooms there. Then, without asking me, the organizers shifted the venue to New York. Suddenly, we had to change all our plans – flights, hotels, everything. It was stressful.

Next, the prize money was reduced. The organizers said they needed some of it for 'extra costs'. Even stranger, the rules said that if the match ended in a tie, Kasparov would still be the champion. I wasn't sure how that was fair, but there was nothing I could do. The rules weren't mine to change.

I was also learning that World Championship matches weren't just about chess. They were about contracts, travel plans, pressure and even politics. I'd never done anything this big before. I had booked flights myself, invited friends for moral support and didn't even have a proper match contract ready until my father stepped in. He worked on the contract, improved it and got it down on paper, which I had neglected to do.

Meanwhile, Kasparov had a full professional team – coaches, trainers, advisers. And they had done all this before. I was the newcomer, the underdog. But I didn't want to show that I was nervous.

The last straw was that the day I reached New York, I came to know something that surprised me: top player Vladimir Kramnik – and someone I considered a friend – was working with Kasparov's team! I found this out quite accidentally, as they had given me the travel list of all those appearing in the match on both sides. I had known Kramnik for years. We had played many games and even shared a few laughs. I didn't expect him to be helping my opponent. It stung. But I reminded myself: this was a World Championship. People wanted to learn from the best, and Kasparov was the best at the time. While I didn't like the situation, I had to accept it.

As befitted the competition, the match was 20 games long. We played four games each week, with barely any rest. The time control was strict: two hours for the first 40 moves, then one hour for the next 20 and finally 30 minutes for the rest of the game.

The match room was surrounded by glass walls, and the spectators sat just beyond them. People paid extra – five times the usual fee – to watch us play. And the walls weren't soundproof, so sometimes I could hear footsteps, murmurs and even the voices of commentators describing our moves. It was strange and a bit distracting.

The first eight games were draws. I didn't want to take big risks early on. Kasparov was too dangerous to face unprepared, and I wanted to ease into the match.

Then came game 9 – and I struck! I sacrificed a rook for a knight and launched my pawns down the centre of the board like charging soldiers. Kasparov tried to defend, but his position crumbled. He resigned after just 35 moves. I was ahead in the match. It was a proud moment.

But I knew Kasparov wouldn't take that lightly.

In game 10, he came back with fire in his eyes. He slammed his pieces down, leapt from his chair after every move and sometimes even stormed out of the room. It felt like he was trying to shake me up. It worked. I lost the game.

Game 11 didn't go much better. I repeated an opening he had already studied, and he punished me for it. Looking back, I realize I had gotten predictable. In chess, that can be dangerous. If your opponent knows what you are going to do, they can prepare the perfect response.

By game 14, I was trying to fight back. I even declined a draw offer to keep pushing. But Kasparov thrived in complicated positions. He played with cool confidence, like someone watching a snowstorm from inside a warm house. I, on the other hand, ran into time trouble. I made mistakes. And I lost.

Eventually, the match ended. Kasparov had won – 10.5 to 7.5.

It wasn't the ending I had dreamt of. But it taught me lessons I couldn't have learnt any other way.

I learnt that preparation goes beyond the chessboard. It includes your team, your travel, your mindset and how you handle unexpected changes.

I learnt not to be predictable. If your opponent knows what you're doing, they will be ready. You have to keep them guessing.

I learnt that experience matters – but it only comes with time. You can't rush it.

A few weeks later, I bumped into Kramnik in Paris. He gave me a small shrug and a shy smile, as if to say, 'Sorry, nothing personal.' I smiled back. I had bigger things to focus on. I knew I would be back.

That match didn't make me World Champion – but it helped me become one.

Because every champion learns from failure. And every big lesson starts with a big challenge.

VISHY SAYS

BECOMING A CHAMPION ISN'T JUST ABOUT PLAYING WELL – IT'S ABOUT FACING TOUGH CHALLENGES, SURPRISES AND EVEN SETBACKS. SOMETIMES THINGS DON'T GO YOUR WAY, AND THAT'S OKAY – EVERY LOSS TEACHES YOU SOMETHING IMPORTANT.

THE SECRET IS TO KEEP LEARNING, KEEP TRYING AND NEVER GIVE UP. BECAUSE EVERY CHAMPION GROWS STRONGER BY TURNING CHALLENGES INTO LESSONS, WHICH ARE THE FOUNDATION FOR EVERYTHING THAT COMES NEXT. SOMETIMES THE HARDEST MATCHES, AND CIRCUMSTANCES, ARE THE ONES THAT MAKE YOU STRONGER.

30

GAMES PEOPLE PLAY

Sometimes, you know the rules of a game aren't fair – but you still choose to play.

That might sound odd, but it's something many athletes, students and even adults face. You might join a contest, exam or tournament while knowing others have an advantage. The unfairness may be in the rules or in things beyond your control. It feels frustrating, but sometimes you decide to focus on the challenge and give it your best. Not because it's fair, but because you want to test yourself.

In 1997–98, I was in that position. FIDE changed the way challengers for the World Chess Championship were chosen. Instead of the traditional Candidates tournament, they introduced a knockout event. But here's the twist: Anatoly Karpov, the reigning champion, was placed straight into the final. The winner of the knockout in Groningen would have to face him just three days later in Lausanne.

It was shocking. Karpov would be fresh, rested and fully prepared. His challenger would arrive exhausted after weeks of tough matches. It was like making two runners compete – one ready at the starting block fresh, the other arriving after a marathon.

Kasparov called the format a joke and refused to play. Kramnik also withdrew in protest. I could have joined them, but I chose instead to play one match at a time. It was unfair, but saying no to the event just because of a possible final felt wrong.

Sometimes life presents you with imperfect options. If you recall, I was faced with similar unfairness in Mexico against Kramnik in 2007. There, if I played the World Championship, I automatically accepted that if I won in Mexico, I would have to play the match against Kramnik. This was much more fair than what happened in Groningen, where if I accepted to play and I won, then I would be forced to play in Lausanne against this well-rested Karpov. And that was a much more unfair situation because I had only three days in between the two matches, whereas the playing field was in a better situation in 2007.

However, the crux of the matter was that the conditions were not perfectly equal for both competitors. Karpov got a huge privilege while Kramnik was getting a slight one. I listed the balance of both options in Groningen: the prize fund was fantastic, and it was a great tournament. I knew that I would play in Groningen in one second if the final match was not there. Then the question was: if playing the first one obliges you to play the second in the event that you win, what do you do?

I decided to take the option. It was a very nice tournament, and I didn't want to give it up. And once you accept that you are going to play, there's no use telling yourself that it's unfair and this and that. It's better to own your decision. If you play, then fishing for sympathy is a waste of time because it doesn't mean anything in such situations. If you win in sport, there is no *need* to explain yourself – whether what you did was correct or not; people will celebrate the fact that you won. And if you lose, then there is no *point* in explaining yourself because no one is interested. You get something at the board or you don't.

The event in 1997 was held in two cities, which helped reduce the intensity a little. With Karpov not there, it was easier to ignore the unfairness. My first match against the Bosnian player Predrag Nikolić went smoothly. Then came the Russian GM Alexander Khalifman, and suddenly I was in trouble. In one game, I was completely lost. My inner voice screamed, 'If I lose this, it's over.' Then, unexpectedly, Khalifman offered me a draw. I accepted instantly. To this day, I don't know why he did it – maybe he misjudged me, maybe he misread his own position. All I knew was that I had escaped. In the tie-break, I managed to win.

That escape gave me energy. I went on to beat Zoltán Almási, a Hungarian GM, Alexei Shirov and Boris Gelfand – all without needing tie-breaks. Each victory not only pushed me further but also doubled the prize money. By the later rounds, one match could equal a whole year's earnings on the chess circuit. No wonder every game felt like life or death. Even coffee breaks seemed like part of the battle.

In the final, I faced English GM Michael Adams. Over four games, I usually had the better positions, but both of us were drained. We'd been playing almost every day in December, and the holiday season gave everything a strange feel. Taxis were scarce, so Adams and I sometimes even shared rides to the venue – competitors yet companions in exhaustion.

The match was close. Adams was stubborn and hard to defeat. Finally, after nine rapid-play tie-break games, I won the right to face Karpov. That's when the real problems began.

We hadn't booked travel to Lausanne because we weren't sure of reaching the final. Flights were full, but a FIDE official told us, 'Once you get to Lausanne, we'll take care of everything.' Aruna smiled: 'If we can get there, we can handle the rest.' But FIDE could easily have bought a few tickets and reserved a hotel room because they knew that one person would be qualifying and would need that assistance. Somehow, we found seats on a flight.

When we landed, we discovered that no hotel had been arranged for me – the finalist who had just survived 21 days of knockout chess. We scrambled to manage basics while the biggest match of my career was just days away. I quickly phoned GM Artur Yusupov in Germany and Leko in Hungary; both agreed to join my team. My long-time trainer, Ubilava, had been with me through Groningen, but I needed more support for this final battle.

***

The match with Karpov was tense. He struck first and led by one point after five games. In the sixth and final game, I decided to take a gamble. I played the Trompowsky – an unusual, attacking opening. It worked. I won, tying the score 3–3 and forcing a rapid-play tie-break.

But weeks of tough matches, travel problems and constant stress had probably taken their toll, and I fell to pieces in a good position. Karpov won and kept his title.

The loss hurt – not because I played badly, but because the odds were stacked against me, and I had come so close. Yet, in chess as in life, something counts only if it's in the bag.

Still, the decision had been mine, and I also learnt something important. Sometimes you choose to play an unfair game after weighing the decision, and once you have decided, you stick with it, accept the outcome and move on.

I was ready to go ahead full throttle.

VISHY SAYS

LIFE MAY OFTEN FORCE YOU TO DEAL WITH IMPERFECT AND UNPLEASANT OPTIONS – LEARNING TO EVALUATE THE PROS AND CONS IS AN IMPORTANT LIFE SKILL. IF YOU FEEL APPREHENSIVE OR HESITANT ABOUT A DECISION, WHERE THE ODDS MAY BE STACKED AGAINST YOU, BUT THEN YOU DECIDE TO GO AHEAD WITH IT, THEN DON'T GO AHEAD IN TWO MINDS. OWN YOUR DECISION, AND GIVE IT YOUR BEST SHOT. OR DON'T DO IT. BUT DOING IT IN TWO MINDS MAKES NO SENSE.

31

ON FITNESS

I didn't really think of it as 'fitness' when I was 13 or 14 years old, but I had already started being active. My father worked in the Railways, and we lived in a place with a huge compound. I would run laps around it at least four times a week.

Later, when I began travelling for tournaments, I walked a lot in the different cities I visited. Everyone has their own reason for exercising – some want to lose weight, others dream of living to a hundred and one! For me, it's about staying active, building stamina and keeping fit. In chess, you need to sit and concentrate for hours, so stamina really matters when you must stay calm and focused for a long game.

It's important to enjoy what you do, so try different activities to keep it fun and interesting. Fitness doesn't have to feel like a punishment. I enjoy running, cycling and even mountain biking. For the last 30 years, I've kept a routine that mixes cardio, weights, gym exercises, and yoga for flexibility. I'm fairly disciplined, so sticking to this isn't too hard – though sometimes I can't resist sweets!

One of the most important things is keeping your mind fresh. Switching to a different topic or activity helps. And of course, the real magic trick for fitness is simple: good, sound sleep.

VISHY SAYS

FITNESS IS LESS ABOUT PUSHING HARD AND MORE ABOUT SHOWING UP, EVERY DAY.

32

ON TOP OF THE WORLD

Sometimes all it takes is one moment to change how you see yourself. For me, that moment came in Wijk aan Zee, a small town in the Netherlands known for its famous chess tournament.

I was still recovering from a tough loss in a World Championship match under very difficult and unfair conditions, when I heard something that made me sit up and decide: I have to win a world title. Nothing else matters now.

While I had played round after round in a gruelling tournament, my opponent, Karpov, had been placed directly into the final without playing earlier rounds. Then Karpov made a comment suggesting I didn't have what it took to win a world title. Hearing that was frustrating. I thought, 'Well, maybe I don't have the "strength of character" to relax on a beach chair while being handed an easy path to the finals! Still, his words stuck with me – and strangely, they helped. They made me more determined than ever to become World Champion.

Around this time, some people suggested I see a sports psychologist. Aruna encouraged me too. I gave it a try and went to one session, but didn't feel comfortable opening up to a stranger about something so personal, so we left it at that.

What helped more than anything was watching a rival succeed.

In 2000, Vladimir Kramnik defeated Garry Kasparov in the World Championship match in London. I found it deeply impressive – not just because of the win, but because of how Kramnik played. He used the Berlin Defence, a solid opening, and caught Kasparov off guard. Just when Kasparov thought he'd figured it out, Kramnik switched things up. He played to win, and did it very intelligently.

Later, Kramnik said that when he helped Kasparov prepare against me in 1995, he didn't think I had a clear strategy. I was predictable. That stung, but I couldn't deny there was some truth in it.

For a long time, I had been happy just being a strong player. I enjoyed travelling, competing and being known as one of the best. I was proud to be the first Indian, and the first Asian, to achieve many things in chess.

But something changed after my 1995 match against Kasparov in New York. That match taught me hard lessons. I had managed to break our streak of eight draws by winning a game – but then I lost control. Kasparov figured me out, and I couldn't recover. From that moment, I knew I had to change how I prepared. I needed to be flexible, surprise my opponents and stay calm under pressure.

Most importantly, I had to want the title of World Champion badly enough.

By the time the next opportunity came, I was ready.

In 2000, the FIDE World Championship was split into two legs. The first part was held in New Delhi, India – my home country. I was thrilled. An Indian IT company – which was also my personal sponsor – NIIT, sponsored the event. I told myself: 'This is your chance.'

The format was a knockout tournament – two-game matches, with faster tie-breaks if needed. I played well through most of the event, but in the quarter-finals, I ran into trouble – again against Khalifman.

It happened on my birthday – 11 December. We ended up playing four rapid tie-break games that day. In one game, I was slipping but somehow wriggled out of trouble. After I won, Veselin Topalov joked, 'Vishy should be called the snake of Madras, not the tiger!' That escape gave me a big confidence boost.

I beat Khalifman in the next game, then defeated Michael Adams in the semi-final.

Now, it was time for the final. The second leg was held in Tehran, Iran. When we arrived, both my coach, Ubilava, and I were completely drained. We had played non-stop chess for weeks, and to make things worse, we both had upset stomachs.

But Aruna had a surprise. She had arranged for our friend and training partner, Pablo San Segundo Carrillo, to join us. He arrived just an hour after we did. Pablo was a great friend and a big help during preparation.

In the final, I faced Alexei Shirov – a brilliant and dangerous player. He had beaten me earlier that year and had defeated Kramnik in a match back in 1998.

Before the match, a Spanish ambassador came to wish Shirov luck. Pumping his fists, he said loudly in Spanish, '*¡Dale bien!* Give him good!' He didn't realize I could understand every word. Shirov, a bit embarrassed, explained that I was as familiar with Spanish as he was. We all laughed later.

When the games began, something was different. Despite the tension and high stakes, I felt calm. Maybe it was the preparation, maybe the years of close calls and hard lessons – but I was ready. The first game was a draw. Then I won the next three in a row.

Suddenly, it was over. I was the World Champion.

When I called Nieves to tell her the news, she laughed joyfully and said, 'Tell your dad I want my money!' She had made a bet with my father four years earlier that I would become World Champion (when he had declared I never would!). And I had waited a long time for this moment too – five years since New York – and every game in between had led here.

VISHY SAYS

SOMETIMES ALL IT TAKES IS ONE MOMENT TO CHANGE HOW YOU SEE YOURSELF. AFTER FACING TOUGH LOSSES AND UNFAIR CHALLENGES, IT'S NORMAL TO FEEL FRUSTRATED. BUT THAT'S WHEN DETERMINATION MATTERS MOST. SUCCESS COMES FROM LEARNING HARD LESSONS, BEING FLEXIBLE AND STAYING CALM UNDER PRESSURE – HELPING YOU GET READY FOR YOUR OWN BIG MOMENT TO SHINE.

33

THE GIFT AND THE GRIT

When I finally won the World Championship in 2000, it wasn't just about those final games in Tehran. It was about everything that had come before. Every stumble, every harsh word, every match I had lost – they all built me up for that moment. Being strong and talented wasn't enough. I had to want it deeply. I had to work harder, prepare smarter, stay calm under pressure and never stop believing that winning was possible.

That journey taught me something valuable I want to share with you.

Have you ever been told you are talented? Maybe you're quick with numbers, a natural artist or fast on the field. It feels good when people notice, doesn't it? But here's what I learnt from chess: talent is only the beginning. What really matters is what you do with it.

My journey from being a young chess player in India to challenging legends around the world was full of passion, practice, failures and some extraordinary wins. But most of all, it showed me that talent needs a teammate: hard work.

When I started playing seriously, I wasn't your typical champion. Most top players then came from the Soviet Union, where chess was everywhere: in parks, schools, even on trains. India didn't have that kind of chess culture. So, to many, I was an outsider – a curious surprise from far away. Even my name didn't sound like theirs. Yet, by the early 1990s, I was challenging the best Soviet players – and even defeating some of them.

When I was young, people often called me 'talented'. At first, it felt like a compliment. But I realized something important: people call you talented when they don't see you as a real threat. The moment I started winning against big names like Kasparov and Karpov, the compliments stopped. Critics arrived. That's when I learnt that being talented wasn't enough. I needed something more.

Talent is like a seed. You might be born with it, but unless you water it – with practice, patience and persistence – it won't grow. Without hard work, talent stays small and unnoticed.

Some people think talent means you don't have to work hard. Others say hard work is more important. I believe both matter. You need the gift. But you also need the grit. A plant doesn't grow just because the seed is strong. It grows when you give it sunlight, water and care. That's what hard work does for talent – it helps it bloom.

When I was growing up, I played super-fast chess, called 'blitz'. It came naturally to me. I was quick at spotting patterns and making moves, which is what earned me the nickname 'Lightning Kid'. But speed has its downsides. Sometimes I made fast moves and fell into traps. I had to train myself to slow down, study tough situations and think carefully. That was hard, but necessary.

It reminded me of the great Indian mathematician Srinivasa Ramanujan. He had no formal training, but his ideas were brilliant. Like him, I was mostly self-taught in a field where most people followed a set path. I had to figure out a lot on my own.

***

Over the years, I've seen many young players start strong and then fade away. Take Joshua Waitzkin, an American chess prodigy whose life inspired the film *Searching for Bobby Fischer.* He was amazing but later moved on to martial arts. Sometimes people leave a pursuit not because they aren't talented, but because their hearts aren't in it anymore. The trick is to find where your true passion lies and then work hard at it.

Even though I showed promise early on, my real breakthrough didn't come until 1983. That year, I won important tournaments in Tamil Nadu, topped the National Sub-Juniors and qualified for the World Championship cycle. I stood out not just because of talent, but because of all the practice and hours of blitz chess.

There are usually two kinds of chess players (besides the banyans and palms!). One group, like the Soviet players, follows a structured path. They study openings, analyse games deeply and train from a young age. The other group, like me, comes from countries without such systems. We play freely, learn by experience and figure things out while playing.

Both styles have their strengths and weaknesses. The first group struggles with chaos. The second group often lacks formal training and learns structure later. The best players learn to do both.

Look at Bobby Fischer. He wasn't just born a genius. He worked extremely hard. He learnt Russian just to read Soviet chess magazines. He studied games from the 1800s. His talent was real – but his success came from obsession, focus and effort.

That's the secret. Talent gives you a head start. Hard work takes you to the finish line.

Throughout my career, there were times I felt stuck. Players I had once beaten easily suddenly got ahead. It was tempting to take it easy. But I didn't. I trained harder, read tournament journals, studied other players' games, tried new ideas and learnt from mistakes.

So, what does it take to succeed? Yes, talent. But also:

- Hard work, to improve what you already have.
- Discipline, to keep going when progress is slow.
- Smart thinking, to train the right way, not just more.
- Curiosity, to learn from everyone and everywhere.
- Luck, for the right doors to open at the right time.

The more you work, the more luck seems to follow.

In the end, I love chess. Okay, once or twice, in a really bad fix, I might have *thought* I hated it, but I've never wanted to quit. Sure, I've had ups and downs, but every break made me return with new energy. That's how I know this is my true passion.

Whether it's chess, music, science or sports – find what you love. Then work at it. Respect your gift, but don't depend on it alone. Talent may start the journey, but hard work wins the game.

And one must not to forget that at any time, an unexpected game-changing force may change everything completely – as happened with the rise of computers in chess.

VISHY SAYS

TALENT GIVES A GREAT START, BUT IT'S HARD WORK THAT REALLY MAKES A DIFFERENCE. LIKE A SEED NEEDS WATER AND SUNSHINE, YOUR SKILLS NEED PRACTICE AND PATIENCE TO GROW. EVERYONE FACES SETBACKS, BUT WHAT MATTERS IS STICKING WITH IT AND LEARNING ALONG THE WAY. WHETHER IT'S CHESS, SPORTS OR ANYTHING ELSE, FINDING WHAT YOU LOVE AND WORKING AT IT IS THE KEY. TALENT GETS YOU GOING, BUT GRIT TAKES YOU ALL THE WAY.

34

HUMOUR HELPS

Humour is one of the best ways to cope when things get tough. It can lift you up when something is pulling you down. For me, watching a stand-up comedy show is a great way to stop worrying too much about the chessboard and just laugh.

I also remember how much fun it was when my mother and her brothers would joke and tease each other. That kind of family humour always makes me feel at home and reminds me not to take everything too seriously.

Humour helps you enjoy the moment and see things in a new light. So don't forget to laugh – it can make even hard times feel easier.

VISHY SAYS

A LITTLE LAUGH CAN MAKE TOUGH TIMES EASIER TO GET PAST.

COOL, WHAT?! I GOT TO BE 'TOP GUN' AT THE OPENING CEREMONY OF THE AMBER TOURNAMENT IN MONACO IN 1999

35

TO BOLDLY GO...

Chess is often called a game of memory, imagination and nerves. Sometimes you don't just need to remember the moves – you have to recall the feelings, patterns and ideas behind them. And sometimes all you have is a faint spark of memory and the clock ticking loudly.

In January 2013, at the famous Wijk aan Zee tournament in the Netherlands, I faced one of those moments. Wijk aan Zee is one of the oldest and most respected chess tournaments. The cold North Sea wind cuts through your coat, the little town smells of coffee and fried fish, and inside the playing hall, some of the best minds in the world quietly fight over 64 squares.

Across from me sat Levon Aronian – the defending champion, World No. 2 and one of the most imaginative players in modern chess. He could make a game feel like stepping into an art gallery, where every beautiful painting also hid a trap.

The position on the board stirred something deep in my memory. My team and I had studied this opening in great detail during my 2012 World Championship match against Boris Gelfand. Back then, we had prepared a very specific idea – like a secret treasure map. It was one of my best ideas for the 2012 match, and now, a few months later, I had the opportunity to apply it.

But now, I couldn't recall the map. My memory was cloudy. I only had one clue: my knight needed to reach the d3 square. Why? I couldn't remember. How? I couldn't recall. It was like knowing a hidden door was in the forest but only remembering a crooked tree nearby.

In chess, the 'main lines' are like wide, safe highways. Now that road seemed blocked. I didn't have the choice to play something safe or define the right moves for the knight. I had to trust my faint memory about the knight and hope the rest would appear along the way.

It was a very sharp position where a single mistake could be fatal. I was guided by the knowledge that my position was good, just that I couldn't remember why. And so I had to work it out by logic, by elimination, and little fragments I could recollect of what was the correct thing to do.

For half an hour, I stitched together scraps of memory and logic. I replayed old mental files – positions, games, half-remembered ideas. Somewhere in the mix, I remembered a famous game I'd seen as a teenager, played in Poland nearly a hundred years earlier, where a knight tore through the enemy's position while bishops lit up the board like searchlights. The similarity between that old game and my position was strangely close.

Then, suddenly, it clicked. I saw a bold bishop sacrifice – daring, surprising and exact. It would open a long diagonal and set my pieces rushing forward. Without hesitation, I played it.

I saw the change on Aronian's face at once – just a tiny flicker, but enough. He realized danger was racing toward his king. I followed it with a knight sacrifice. On the scoresheet, it looked like I was throwing pieces away. On the board, it was the start of a trap snapping shut.

A few moves later, the dust cleared. My queen was perfectly placed, my bishops dominated the board, and Aronian's king was surrounded. Checkmate was certain.

Victory.

The satisfaction wasn't only in winning; it was in fighting through doubt and coming out ahead. It felt like cooking a dish from memory, forgetting half the ingredients, inventing the rest and still ending up with something delicious. Once I found the right idea, everything connected, and I was able to play out the idea and play a fantastic game.

For me, it was one of the most beautiful games of my career – not because of exact preparation, but because of the leap of faith. Trusting my instincts and letting my imagination take over carried me exactly where I needed to be.

Chess isn't just a battle of pieces; it's a long fight of patience, memory and nerves. Even the best preparation can vanish when you need it most. That's when you rely on the base you've built – small clues you remember, patterns you recognize and the sense of what 'feels right' in a position.

But the game also whispered a warning. Chess was changing fast. Computers and engines were rising, and the next generation of 'secret maps' would be drawn not just by human memory but by machines that could calculate millions of positions every second. Preparation was becoming less about remembering exact sequences and more about steering the game into positions where you – not the computer – felt at home.

That day in Wijk aan Zee taught me important lessons about control and risk.

VISHY SAYS

WE MAY WANT TO KEEP MEMORIZING THINGS SO THAT NOTHING MAY GO WRONG AND WE ARE ALWAYS IN PERFECT CONTROL. BUT SOMETIMES YOU JUST HAVE TO TAKE THE TOOLS IN YOUR HAND AND FIND THE BEST MOVE. AS LONG AS YOU REMEMBER A FEW KEY IDEAS, APPLY LOGIC, INTUITION AND THE PROCESS OF ELIMINATION – YOU ARE ABLE TO FIND THE SOLUTION (LIKE THE SHERLOCK HOLMES QUOTE: 'WHEN YOU HAVE ELIMINATED THE IMPOSSIBLE, WHATEVER REMAINS, HOWEVER IMPROBABLE, MUST BE THE TRUTH').

HOWEVER WELL PREPARED YOU ARE, DON'T EXPECT TO ALWAYS BE IN CONTROL OF THE SITUATION – LIFE IS VERY UNPREDICTABLE. SOME RISK WILL ALWAYS BE THERE.

36

THE NEW GIANT ON THE BLOCK

The year FIDE officially conferred the title of Grandmaster on me – 1988 – was also the year I first used a computer to prepare for chess. I got my first computer as a gift in 1987, but since I couldn't bring it into India right away, it stayed with a friend in Amsterdam while the permission papers were processed. It took about eight months before I could finally fly home with it. Back then, there was no special chess software on the computer, so I just typed moves one by one. Only later, when I visited a friend named Frederic, who had developed chess software, did I realize how important the right programs were for making the computer truly useful.

Late that year, I bought a laptop – huge and heavy by today's standards! The best part was that suddenly all my chess books and notes could fit inside one machine. I no longer had to carry heavy books to tournaments. But getting the laptop through Customs at the airport was a nightmare. The officials wanted to charge me a huge tax because the computer wasn't only for chess –

it could be used to type letters too! Thankfully, I was finally able to get it home.

I was part of the first group of players to use computers seriously for chess. The famous chess database program ChessBase was just an idea when I met its creator, Frederic, in 1987. He was excited to show me how it worked and invited me to his home in Germany to use it. I was nervous at first but soon got used to it – and even taught Frederic some corrections after spotting errors in the games stored on the program.

Over time, computers started to change the game in big ways. At first, chess engines – the programs that analyse positions and suggest moves – were very weak. They only helped by pointing out basic mistakes, like a calculator checking your maths homework. But slowly, these engines grew stronger and started finding moves even the best players missed.

One of the biggest moments was when IBM's Deep Blue computer beat the World Champion Garry Kasparov in 1997. This shocked many people outside the chess world, but for us players, it was just a sign that computers were catching up. We knew humans still had strengths computers didn't, at least back then.

I remember playing a special match in 1999 where I teamed up with a computer to play against former World Champion Karpov and his computer. It showed how important it was to learn how to work with these new tools. Karpov struggled because he wasn't used to computers, while I had grown up using them.

Today, chess players rely on computers for preparation, but it's still important to understand the ideas behind the moves – not just memorize endless data. Sometimes too much information without understanding can be confusing rather than helpful.

During the 2007 World Championship, my team tried something new: we let our computers play against each other overnight to test opening ideas. This gave us fresh inspiration and confidence. But technology can have its quirks – while we were watching a funny movie during a break in this very important tournament, my computer overheated and froze! We had to cool it down in front of the air conditioner to get it working again!

This was very different from the 2010 World Championship in Sofia. Back then, there was a scary rumour that my opponent, Topalov, had a supercomputer with 112 cores – a super-powerful machine running a strong chess program called Rybka 4. I couldn't even imagine how much help such a machine could give him because I had never worked with anything that strong. But what we didn't realize was that it's not just about how powerful a computer is – it's about how well the software can use that power.

It's like having a faster car: does it take you somewhere new, or does it just get you there quicker? A faster car that doesn't take you somewhere different is just a faster car. The same idea applies to computers – they can be faster, but they might not show you anything new.

When it comes to information, having too much isn't always good. It can confuse you. Some of the best games I've played happened when I had only a little information but a clear goal. It's better to have a few pieces of correct information than a lot that may leave you confused.

For example, in August 2017, I played against American GM Fabiano Caruana at the Sinquefield Cup in St. Louis. I surprised him by choosing the English Opening, which I don't use very often. Caruana played a move I didn't know well, so I had to rely on my instincts and experience instead of data or preparation. Even though his rook was threatening my queen, I kept attacking his king. The last move was my queen moving to a square where Caruana's rook could capture it – but he missed it! That move won me the game. It was one of my prettiest games, even though I didn't have special preparation.

Now, with artificial intelligence (AI) in chess, things are changing even more. AI is like a super-smart computer that learns by playing itself, without humans telling it what to do. One AI program, AlphaZero, learnt chess from just the rules in four hours – and then it beat the strongest chess engine, Stockfish, in 1,000 games!

What makes AI amazing is that it can teach itself to play in a way that removes human mistakes or biases. It shows us new ideas and hidden tricks that old computers only showed if we knew exactly where to look. AI is opening new doors in chess and making the game exciting again.

With AI, we get loads of new information, and we have to learn how to understand and use it well. Instead of rejecting new ideas just because they seem strange or accepting them blindly, we need to keep an open mind and be willing to change. That's the best way to stay ahead in chess.

My coach, Grzegorz Gajewski, started using AI tools before I did, and he was so impressed that I had to try it too. Now, we use both old programs and AI. Sometimes they disagree, and that's when I learn the most!

These days, I can run an AI engine on my computer, do something else like watch a movie and then come back to see what it has discovered. My job is to understand these new ideas in detail and add them to my skills.

Right now, chess is going through big changes. New players might see the board in ways we never imagined. Thanks to AI, anyone with a computer can learn like the best players. And children can play through games without even a chessboard.

The important questions are: What new things can I learn? What old ideas should I forget? What do I understand well enough to use in my games?

It won't be easy, but it's exciting!

The best way to succeed, whether in chess or life, is to be open to change. We all have skills and ideas that worked before, but things change. Being willing to learn, adapt and let go of old biases will help you grow and win.

Chess, like life, keeps changing. Computers and AI have made it a new and exciting game full of surprises. The winners won't just be the smartest or strongest players – they will be the ones who keep learning, stay curious and are brave enough to try new things. That's how you become a true champion!

VISHY SAYS

THE WORLD AROUND US IS ALWAYS CHANGING, OFTEN FASTER THAN WE EXPECT. SUCCESS DOESN'T COME FROM SIMPLY COLLECTING MORE INFORMATION OR CLINGING TO OLD HABITS. WHAT REALLY MATTERS IS HOW WILLING YOU ARE TO KEEP LEARNING, TO STAY CURIOUS AND TO ADAPT WHEN THINGS SHIFT. WHETHER IT'S SCHOOL, SPORTS OR LIFE ITSELF, THE REAL CHAMPIONS ARE THE ONES WHO STAY OPEN-MINDED AND BRAVE ENOUGH TO TRY NEW THINGS.

37

THE THINKING GAME

When I was a boy, I loved playing blitz chess. The kind where you had only five minutes on the clock – and every second mattered. I moved fast, trusted my instincts and won a lot of games that way. I wore the title 'Lightning Kid' proudly.

But speed, I would learn, can be both a gift and a trap. And rushing doesn't always win, even in a game of speed.

I had always believed that my quick thinking was my greatest strength. While others took long pauses, I would zip through my moves. I felt confident, even unstoppable. But the more serious my opponents became, the more I realized that speed alone wasn't enough. Blitz games may reward instinct, but tournament games demand depth.

At first, it was hard to change. I was used to winning with my natural style – sharp, fast, tactical. But chess at the highest level wasn't about the flashiest move. It was about finding the *right* move, even if it took time. And that was something I had to learn the hard way, such as during a match against Garry Kasparov in 1995.

I had a winning position. Everything was going well. But instead of taking time to calculate fully, I trusted my first idea and played quickly. The move looked strong – but it wasn't. Kasparov turned the game around, and I lost. The sting of that mistake stayed with me. I kept thinking, 'Why didn't I just pause and double-check?'

Of course, I was already training myself differently. I practised going deeper into positions, looking beyond my first impulse. I tried to enjoy the slower pace, to find satisfaction in analysing every possibility. It wasn't easy – my mind wanted to race ahead – but I knew I had to change.

Some habits are hard to break. When you have played thousands of fast games, your brain gets wired a certain way. I had to unlearn bad habits like playing automatically or assuming too soon that I knew the answer. I started asking myself more questions during games: 'What is my opponent thinking? What could I be missing? Is this really the best move or just the fastest one?'

One of the things that had helped along the way was 'visualization'. I trained myself to 'see' the board in my mind – what it would look like five or six moves ahead. Sometimes I would read games without a board and try to imagine all the moves just by reading the notation. This helped me slow down and sharpen my imagination.

Over time, I started to appreciate the beauty of deeper thinking. It was like turning a simple puzzle into a rich story. Every move had a reason. Every plan had layers.

And this didn't just help me in chess. It helped me in life too.

Because thinking carefully isn't just for chess players. It's useful when solving a tricky maths problem, deciding how to respond in an argument or choosing what to say in an exam. Chess teaches you patience, planning and self-control – qualities that can shape how you think in everyday life.

Even today, I enjoy a good blitz game once in a while. But I've learnt that the best moves aren't always the fastest ones. The real skill lies in knowing when to trust your instinct – and when to stop and think.

That was a strength I needed most definitely while facing the giants, the best in the world.

***

When I began competing with the world's top players, I was curious: 'What made them great? What did they know that I didn't? And what would it take for me to match them?'

In those early years, I was often the youngest player in the room. My opponents were Grandmasters with years of experience. Their names were known around the world – Karpov, Kasparov, Korchnoi. They had fought battles I had only read about.

At first, it was intimidating. But I saw every game as a lesson.

One of the biggest learnings was this: to beat the best, you have to understand them. Not fear them, not copy them – but truly understand how they think. Before important matches, I'd study my opponents carefully. I'd look at the openings they preferred, the positions they enjoyed and the kinds of mistakes they made. Each player had patterns, and if you spotted them, you could prepare well.

But preparation wasn't just about knowing your opponent – it was about knowing yourself.

I once tried copying the style of another top player. It didn't work. I realized I couldn't just fit myself into someone else's game. I had to build my own. For me, that meant keeping my natural sharpness, but adding new layers of thought – more planning, more structure, more discipline. I tried to include a mental checklist before I trusted my instinct and made the move that I liked. I still trusted my eyes and instincts, but there was only advantage in giving the conclusions one quick stress test.

Slowly, I began to grow as a player. I stopped being just the fast kid and became someone who could handle complex positions. I started winning against players I had admired for years.

Still, there were tough moments.

***

I remember my early games against Anatoly Karpov. He was a former World Champion – calm, steady and extremely hard to beat. The first few times we played, I felt the pressure. But over time, I reminded myself: he's just another player; the board is the same for both of us. Once I started focusing on the *game*, not the *name*, my results improved.

Even losses became important lessons. Losing to a great player didn't make me feel small. It made me curious. I would go back to the game, study every move and ask, 'Where did I go wrong?' I wasn't just collecting wins; I was collecting knowledge.

Of course, nothing tested me more than facing Garry Kasparov.

He was fierce, fast and frighteningly prepared. Playing against him felt like stepping into a storm. You had to be ready for anything. For my 1995 World Championship match against him, I trained harder than ever. I studied his games, prepared new openings, worked with a team of strong trainers and built strategies that were just for him.

Even though I didn't win that match, it was a turning point in my career. I had taken on the best and held my ground. I had learnt what it meant to prepare at the highest level – and I knew I'd come back stronger.

That experience also taught me the value of smart training. It's not just about how long you practise, but *how* you practise. Don't just keep doing what you're already good at. Work on your weak spots. Understand the logic behind every move. Focus on the quality, not just the quantity.

Chess, I realized, isn't about being perfect. It's about improving every day. It's about becoming stronger by asking questions, facing challenges and being willing to change.

Even when you're up against a giant, you always have one secret weapon: your mind. It can take you through to a win.

And if it doesn't, it can definitely help you deal with the aftermath.

VISHY SAYS

IT'S EXCITING TO ACT FAST, BUT RUSHING OFTEN CAUSES MISTAKES. THE SMARTEST CHOICES USUALLY HAPPEN WHEN YOU PAUSE AND THINK CAREFULLY. TAKING A MOMENT TO IMAGINE WHAT COULD HAPPEN NEXT – AND ASKING YOURSELF QUESTIONS LIKE, *'IS THIS REALLY THE BEST THING TO DO?'* – CAN MAKE ALL THE DIFFERENCE. IN SCHOOL, AT HOME OR WITH FRIENDS, PATIENCE AND PLANNING USUALLY LEAD TO BETTER RESULTS THAN CHARGING AHEAD WITHOUT THINKING.

38

A MUSTER OF MENTORS

When I think of my first 'guides', I don't have to look far – it was my parents. My mother especially set the rules early on. My brother and sister were much older, so they also watched out for me. At school too I learnt how far I could push before teachers or friends got annoyed – that was my first lesson in putting up guard rails!

I often copied the way my parents and siblings behaved. Of course, we didn't always agree – we sometimes argued strongly – but in the end, we always found a solution. One of the most important lessons my mother gave me was never to make hasty decisions. That advice proved priceless later, when I was playing tense World Championship matches.

As I grew older, I had many different kinds of mentors. Mauricio Perea, or Maurice, and his wife, Nieves, for example, weren't chess coaches in the usual sense, but they were like an extra set of parents for me. They gave me confidence, belief and a sense of stability when I was young and competing abroad. Without them, it would have been much tougher for me to adjust and do well internationally.

Then there were my 'seconds' – the special team members who helped me prepare for matches. I never saw them as assistants but as true allies. Their support gave me strength and courage during the most high-pressure games. Just knowing that people were behind me made me feel stronger.

VISHY SAYS

HAVING MENTORS IS LIKE HAVING A SAFETY NET – THEY CHEER YOU ON, GUIDE YOU AND GIVE YOU THAT LITTLE PUSH WHEN YOU NEED IT MOST. NEVER UNDERESTIMATE HOW IMPORTANT IT IS TO HAVE PEOPLE IN YOUR CORNER. AND ONE DAY, YOU MIGHT BE THAT MENTOR FOR SOMEONE ELSE!

39

LOSING HURTS, BUT IT'S NOT THE END

Even champions lose. And when they do, it hurts deeply. But what matters more than the loss is what comes after.

Most people think champions are used to winning – and maybe even used to losing. But that's not true. When you lose something important, it's always painful.

In 2013, I played Magnus Carlsen in the World Chess Championship and lost my title. That match was one of the toughest experiences of my career – not just because I lost, but because I felt slow, tired and helpless throughout. Nothing I tried seemed to work. And the worst part came after the final game, when I had to sit at a press conference, facing dozens of reporters, trying to explain my mistakes – when I hadn't even figured them out myself.

There's a strange silence that comes after a loss. It's not just outside you. It's inside too. You go quiet. You question everything. And you feel alone, even when others are around.

This wasn't the first time I had felt that way. Years earlier, in a tournament in Dortmund, I lost a game to Vladimir Kramnik. I resigned early and left the playing hall without saying much. I walked for hours through the city, trying to clear my head. My thoughts were racing, my heart heavy. Even though I'd won many tournaments before and would go on to win many more, in that moment, I felt like I didn't belong at the top anymore. That's what a tough loss can do – it can shake your belief in yourself.

The thing about losing in public is that everyone sees it. The cameras catch your reaction. The journalists ask sharp questions. People online post opinions before you have had a chance to breathe. And you still have to show up, speak clearly and stay calm – even when your mind feels like a storm.

Over the years, I've realized that losing with grace is also a skill. It takes maturity to admit you were outplayed, to accept it without excuses and to face the world with honesty. You can't always control the result, but you can control how you respond. Even when it feels awful.

After the Carlsen match, I started to doubt myself more than ever before. I asked questions I'd never dared to ask: 'Am I still good enough? Have I passed my peak? Will I ever play that well again?' These thoughts are hard to shake. But they are also a normal part of the journey. What matters is what you do next.

For me, it helped to step away from the chessboard for a while. I spent time with my family, read books, played with my son and let myself enjoy small things again. Slowly, the pain faded. Slowly, the pressure lifted.

Slowly, I began to want to play again – not to prove anything, but because I missed the game.

And mistakes? I've made plenty – some small, some embarrassing and some that cost me entire tournaments.

One still makes me laugh now, though it wasn't funny at the time. It was the final round of a tournament. I had just played a clever move that forced my opponent to resign. I was pleased. I even signed the scoresheet and stood up. But as I walked away, someone whispered, 'Anand, your rook was hanging.'

What? I went back and looked. They were right! My rook was sitting unprotected. If my opponent had noticed and played one simple move, I would have lost instantly. But he hadn't. He thought I had seen something brilliant – and gave up too soon. I escaped with a win, but the truth was hard to ignore: I had made a silly, careless mistake. No matter how experienced you are, you're never too old – nor too good – to goof up.

Other times, mistakes don't go unnoticed. Once, I played a move I had already decided not to play. That sounds strange, I know. But it happens. Sometimes, under pressure, your hand moves faster than your brain. The moment I made the move, I knew it was wrong. My heart sank. I sat there, still pretending to think, even though I knew the game was over.

Mistakes like that feel awful. You want to rewind time. You want to disappear. But you can't. So, you sit there, accept the result and try to learn what you can from it.

***

Some people feel ashamed of their errors. They avoid thinking about them. They push them aside and hope to forget. But I believe the opposite: you should examine your mistakes closely. Not to punish yourself, but to understand what went wrong: Was it overconfidence? Did you rush? Were you distracted? Did you forget something you already knew? When you understand the reason behind a mistake, you can work to prevent it in the future. That's how progress happens – not by avoiding failure, but by learning from it.

Over time, my blunders taught me to slow down when needed, to double-check ideas and to respect my opponent even when I felt confident. They helped me improve more than my victories ever could.

After my 2013 World Championship loss to Carlsen, I had a choice: give in to disappointment or rebuild myself. The rebuilding took time – and it started with small steps. I didn't suddenly change everything. I just tried to find joy in the game again. Ironically, it began with staying away from chess for two months. Once the memory of my loss faded, the desire to play returned.

By the time the Candidates tournament came in 2014, I felt ready. I played well, stayed focused and even qualified again to challenge for the world title. The confidence returned and I began to trust my instincts again. Even though I didn't win that match either, I felt proud – not just of how I played, but of the person I had become after that earlier loss. I had faced doubt, struggled through setbacks, and come back with strength and calm. That kind of comeback means more to me than any quick win.

There's one moment I'll never forget. After a match, a young boy came up to me and said simply, 'I know you'll come back.' He didn't ask a question. He didn't say it like a fan. He said it like a friend who believed in me. And in that small moment, something inside me shifted.

Sometimes when you're lost in your own thoughts, someone else's belief in you can light the way. It reminds you of your purpose, your passion and your ability to grow beyond any mistake. That child's words stayed with me – quiet but powerful. They reminded me that failure is never final. Resilience is built not in easy victories, but in the hard, slow climb after you fall.

THE THEN PRESIDENT OF INDIA, PRATIBHA PATIL, PRESENTING THE PADMA VIBHUSHAN TO ME AT THE RASHTRAPATI BHAVAN IN 2008...OH, WHAT A FEELING!

Champions aren't perfect. They make mistakes, feel doubt and sometimes lose badly. What makes them different is how they respond. They think things over. They improve. They come back.

I've learnt that the biggest victories aren't always trophies or titles. Sometimes the biggest victory is believing in yourself again after you've failed. So, the next time you make a mistake, don't hide from it. Look at it closely. Understand it. Learn from it. And then keep going. Because every great comeback begins with a single step forward.

Even when challenges pop up out of nowhere.

VISHY SAYS

LOSING CAN STING, BUT EVERYONE LOSES SOMETIMES. IT DOESN'T MEAN YOU'VE FAILED FOREVER. WHAT MATTERS MOST IS HOW YOU RESPOND. INSTEAD OF HIDING FROM MISTAKES, TRY TO UNDERSTAND THEM. ASK YOURSELF WHAT WENT WRONG AND HOW YOU CAN IMPROVE.

TAKING TIME TO HEAL, LEARNING FROM LOSS AND BELIEVING IN YOURSELF AGAIN ARE WHAT HELP YOU GROW STRONGER. ACCEPTING THE SITUATION AND MOVING ON IS THE BEST SOLUTION, BUT IT IS NOT AT ALL EASY TO DO. YOU CAN MAKE THE MENTAL EFFORT TO GO FORWARD. . . OR LET THE PASSING OF TIME DO IT FOR YOU.

40

A CHANCE TO GIVE BACK

Sometimes life takes unexpected turns. For me, 2020 was one of those years. The world changed faster than I ever imagined, and it made me think deeply about my love for chess – and how I could help the next generation of players grow.

In 2020, everything changed.

I had travelled to Germany in February for a big chess tournament called the Bundesliga. Between the games, I went to Warsaw for two weeks of training with my coach, Gajewski. We talked about the new virus spreading fast – COVID-19. It felt like a speeding train coming toward us, but neither of us thought it would stop the whole world so suddenly.

When the pandemic hit, I was stuck in a quiet town called Bad Soden in Germany. Flights were cancelled, and the rest of the tournament was called off. At least I had one thing to look forward to – flying back home to Chennai in a week.

Then India announced a nationwide lockdown. Suddenly, I couldn't leave. I felt restless but tried to be patient. Luckily, I had a job as an online commentator for a big chess tournament happening in Russia. Even as the world shut down, chess games kept going – online.

Looking back, it all felt strange at first. When March turned into April, it didn't seem so bad. The weather was nice in Bad Soden, and I went for walks and runs every day.

But things got worse. The nearby supermarket started asking everyone to wear masks and keep apart. Only 20 people could go inside at once – the rest had to wait outside in line. News from Italy and Spain was scary. Hospitals were full. Back in India, panic grew and lockdowns kept getting longer. No one knew what would happen next.

While waiting to get back home, I had to play in an online chess tournament – the Online Nations Cup. It was a team event with Russia, the USA, India and others. Before the tournament, I felt nervous. I hadn't played serious chess for a whole month and felt out of practice.

I quickly reviewed some games and jumped in. The matches started in the afternoon and lasted about two hours, so I played two games a day. The tournament went well for me, which was a relief.

As time passed, it became clear that the only way home was on a special flight run by the Indian government. I contacted the embassy, filled out forms and finally flew out of Frankfurt.

Seeing everyone on the plane wearing masks and face shields, barely making eye contact, felt like a scene from a science-fiction movie – it was strange and unsettling.

When I got back to India, I had to quarantine for 14 days. I spent the first half in a hotel in Bengaluru and the rest at home in Chennai. It felt strange to be locked in a room, separated from my family by a glass door. During meals, they knocked and left food outside. Thankfully, after a week, I could join them at the dining table again.

Once I was home, I agreed to play in the Legends of Chess tournament, an online event with players from around the world. I almost withdrew but kept delaying the decision until it was too late.

Honestly, I found online tournaments tiring, mostly because of the time difference. Games often started at 8 p.m. and went on until midnight, which messed up my daily routine. My performance was poor – I finished ninth out of ten, with only one win.

The next tournament, the Online Olympiad, was better. India tied with Russia for first place, which was very exciting.

By mid-2020, over-the-board chess tournaments had disappeared. I missed playing face-to-face with real opponents – clicking pieces on a screen wasn't the same. The pandemic stopped almost all sports, including chess.

For older players like me, this break was easier to accept. I didn't have to decide whether to stop playing tournaments – they simply didn't happen.

***

During this time, an idea I had been thinking about for a long while came to life: starting a chess academy.

Back in early 2019, I had been invited by an investment firm in Bengaluru called WestBridge Capital to give a talk for their employees. After the event, Sandeep Singhal, one of the founders, asked if I wanted to do a chess project together.

That was the start of the WestBridge Anand Chess Academy, or WACA.

I was inspired by the Botvinnik Chess School in Moscow. It was started by the former world champion Mikhail Botvinnik and helped train players like Kasparov and Karpov, who later became world champions themselves.

I thought a similar academy in India, where I could mentor young players, would be a great project. We had planned to launch it in April 2020, but the pandemic delayed our plans.

Meanwhile, online chess grew a lot. Chess had always been easy to play online – you just need a computer and an internet connection. During the pandemic, many people learnt and played chess online. Instructional videos and chess content creators helped bring new players to the game.

Also, the Netflix show *The Queen's Gambit* came out. It told a gripping story about chess and made the game even more popular. Almost everyone I knew, even people who didn't play chess, talked about the show. As a player, I could relate to it – it captured the excitement and tension of chess tournaments perfectly.

Because of the show and the rise of online chess, the sport actually grew during the pandemic – which was unusual, since almost every other sport suffered.

At the start of the pandemic, I got involved in online chess mostly as a commentator and player. But I found it tiring to prepare for online events and spend hours on camera. Many top players loved streaming online, but I never fully enjoyed it.

By December 2020, the pandemic was still going strong. Physical tournaments and travel were still impossible. It seemed like the perfect time to start WACA.

WestBridge and I agreed on the academy's goal: to help talented young Indian players develop into world-class champions. We wanted to support them as they moved from being top young players in India to competing with the best in the world.

I was excited about the chance to work with young minds and see the game through their eyes. It was also a way to formalize my friendship with some young players I met sometimes. Most of all, it was my chance to give back to chess – something I had wanted for a long time.

By the time we officially launched in 2021, a few things had changed. Chess was booming online, but I wasn't sure where my own playing career stood. I didn't want to stop competing, but I also didn't want to chase tournaments. The break had been good for me.

The academy fit well into this new phase of my life.

I chose five of the most promising young players – Nihal Sarin, R. Praggnanandhaa, R. Vaishali, Raunak Sadhwani and D. Gukesh – and started creating training courses for them. Teaching someone else forces you to explain concepts clearly, to acknowledge whether you understand them fully yourself. We met online to play games, discuss ideas and analyse matches, and I shared lessons from my own wins and losses.

I invited three of my former coaches – Artur Yusupov, Sandipan Chanda and Grzegorz Gajewski – to join as trainers. Our plan was to regularly check the players' progress and offer new fellowships to talented young players every year.

The pandemic changed the world and my life in ways I never expected. But it also gave me a chance to pause, think, and find new ways to share my love of chess. Helping young players grow and succeed is now one of the most rewarding parts of my life. The game I've loved for so long continues to inspire me – and, I hope, it will inspire a new generation of champions too.

Meanwhile, I had got inspired too.

VISHY SAYS

LIFE CAN CHANGE SUDDENLY AND PLANS MIGHT GET PAUSED OR DISRUPTED. WHEN THAT HAPPENS, FINDING NEW WAYS TO KEEP DOING WHAT YOU LOVE CAN LEAD TO UNEXPECTED OPPORTUNITIES. SUCCESS ISN'T ONLY ABOUT WINNING OR REACHING GOALS – IT'S ALSO ABOUT SHARING YOUR PASSION AND SKILLS, AND HELPING OTHERS GROW. TEACHING AND SUPPORTING OTHERS CAN BRING FRESH ENERGY AND PURPOSE, OPENING NEW PATHS.

41

GIRLS IN CHESS

For a long time, chess had more boys than girls playing. In some places, girls didn't always get enough time, support or training to play chess as much as boys did. Sometimes unkind attitudes made girls feel like chess wasn't for them. That's why there have been fewer girls in chess overall. But things are changing, slowly but surely, and today more girls are picking up the game.

There's a well-known story about Susan Polgár, the Hungarian American grandmaster who was Women's World Champion between 1996 and 1999. She once remarked that she had 'never beaten a completely healthy man' – because whenever she won, some male opponents explained away their loss by saying they had a headache or weren't feeling well. It shows how difficult it could be for women players to be taken seriously. Still, players like her in India and the rest of the world have proved that talent and hard work can silence doubt better than words ever could.

In India, many girls tend to stop playing chess around the time they are 13 or 14 years old, while boys continue to move ahead. The good news is that chess federations and organizations across the world now acknowledge this problem and are taking steps to encourage more girls to stay in the game. With growing support and strong role models, the board is likely to look more balanced in the future.

VISHY SAYS

DON'T LET OTHER PEOPLE'S DOUBTS DECIDE WHAT YOU CAN OR CANNOT DO. IF YOU BELIEVE IN YOURSELF AND KEEP GOING, YOU CAN BREAK BARRIERS – NOT JUST IN CHESS, BUT IN LIFE.

42

WHEN THE WORLD STOPPED

When the pandemic hit, it felt as if the whole world pressed pause. Like everyone else, I was thrown into a strange new life of unstructured days. Tournaments stopped. Travel plans vanished. The busy rhythm of chess came to a sudden halt. My playing career was put on hold without warning or explanation. Strangely, I didn't feel restless. It was simply beyond my control.

Instead, I found comfort in small, steady things – home, routines and family. Even when everyone was on a screen or in different rooms, being together made the uncertainty easier to bear. In a world that seemed to change every hour, family was the one constant.

The pandemic offered two choices: feel stuck and anxious or look for the hidden gift inside the pause – time. With flights grounded and offices closed, life slowed down. I asked myself what I had always wanted to learn but kept putting off. The answer was: Hindi.

The lockdown finally gave me that chance. With help from my friend Ananth Subramaniam in Chicago, I started weekly Skype lessons. Week by week, I grew a little more confident – enough to manage simple conversations at airports or share a quick joke with my teammates. I wasn't fluent, but I was moving forward, and that felt good.

The pandemic didn't just give me time for lessons. It also reminded me of what matters most – family. During those months, I said goodbye to my father, and that loss drew me even closer to the people around me.

***

Being home and not travelling for long stretches meant I could visit my father more often in Besant Nagar. At 92, his memory was fading. Our chats went round in circles, but seeing him once or twice a week felt deeply comforting. He would come over for birthdays and Diwali.

In early April 2021, he fell ill and was admitted to hospital. Because of COVID-19, we couldn't visit. For a few days, the updates swung between hopeful and worrying. On 15 April, the hospital made an emergency call, but he was gone before we could get there. We hadn't managed one last look at him while he was still living.

If my mother was my visible support when I was young, my father worked quietly behind the scenes. He arranged his railway tours to be near tournaments, used his network to sort out travel and made sure I could focus on playing. Because of him, so many practical worries simply disappeared.

In 1984, at my first World Sub-Juniors in France, my parents came along. I stayed in the tournament village;

they stayed with a family friend from the Indian embassy, and took trains and buses to watch me play. One day I felt very drowsy. My father checked my eyes and decided I had jaundice. We didn't want to alert anyone and risk my withdrawal, so he told me to avoid eye contact – look up, down or away, he told me, anything so no one would notice. I did just that!

Three years later, at the Nationals in Tumkur, my start was poor. I acted casual, as if I didn't care. My father thought I was drifting and gave me a stern talk about proving myself. Later, chess legend Manuel Aaron gently advised him that pressure might not help. My father listened. On the rest day, he took me to Bangalore and made peace with me with tall glasses loaded with mango ice cream. After that, I went on a winning run and finished first. Sometimes encouragement looks like a lecture; sometimes it looks like dessert!

In my early career, he also acted as my manager. He spoke to sponsors, came with me to ad shoots and even offered producers his unasked-for ideas. We once travelled to Bombay for an ad and ended up bickering on the way. Looking back, I feel a little sorry about those arguments, but they were natural for that age. He was learning to let go; I was learning to stand on my own.

As he grew older, certain questions became regular. Before any trip, he would ask if I was going to Linares, not remembering the tournament had ended years earlier. Many times, he wondered aloud if I had retired, worried when my name wasn't in the morning paper. 'Oh, you're still playing,' he'd say, surprised. 'Not retired yet?' I would smile and tell him, 'Not yet, Appa.'

Nothing lit him up like stories from his railway days, especially his trips to Zambia and Kenya to discuss wagons and locomotives. He told those tales with pride and a sense of adventure.

His happiest routine in later years was Sunday ice cream with his grandson. We would carry tubs over, and he would watch Akhil steal spoonfuls from everyone. The two of them adored each other. My father lived a long, full life, yet his final days are, for me, tied to the pandemic that kept us from saying goodbye in person. Even though I don't show it often, his absence still feels like a heavy weight on my chest.

Seeing all this as a parent made me feel more strongly about it. I watched Akhil adjust to online school, with his friends turned into tiny squares on a screen. When I was away, I wondered if he remembered to present his science project or smiled when an assignment used something we had practised together. I wanted to be there for him, the way my parents had been there for me.

The pause also opened a new path. Coaching a group of talented young players became a fresh challenge. Teaching is different from playing; it made me prepare more, think from other people's viewpoints and turn old experiences into lessons someone else could use. While tournaments were uncertain, coaching gave me purpose.

When events returned, the long gaps still felt unusual. I had already been thinking about retirement, and the pandemic made me reflect more deeply on what matters. Trophies and rankings will always be part of the story, but they are not the whole story. The world

I knew had changed, and the only way forward was to be open, flexible and willing to find joy in new things.

Life, like chess, needs strategy – but it also needs patience and the courage to change plans when the old ones no longer fit. The pandemic reminded me that even when everything stops, there is still room to grow, to learn and to move forward – one small step at a time.

VISHY SAYS

WHEN LIFE SUDDENLY SLOWS DOWN OR CHANGES IN WAYS YOU CAN'T CONTROL, IT'S EASY TO FEEL STUCK OR LOST. BUT THESE PAUSES CAN ALSO BE A CHANCE TO TRY SOMETHING NEW, LIKE LEARNING A LANGUAGE, PICKING UP A HOBBY OR HELPING OTHERS. SMALL DAILY ROUTINES AND CONNECTIONS WITH FAMILY OR FRIENDS CAN KEEP YOU STEADY THROUGH UNCERTAIN TIMES.

REMEMBER, GROWTH DOESN'T ALWAYS COME FROM BIG MOMENTS BUT FROM SMALL STEPS FORWARD. WHEN THE WORLD STOPS, USE THAT TIME TO DISCOVER NEW PATHS AND KEEP MOVING AHEAD.

43

A CHEAT SHEET

After more than a year away from live chess tournaments, stepping back onto the competitive stage was both exciting and nerve-wracking. The world had changed, and so had the way chess was played. This chapter is the story of my return – the struggles I faced, the surprises along the way, and some important lessons about fairness and honesty that I learnt.

When I first took a break from tournaments, it felt like a temporary pause. But as days turned into months, and months into a year, a strange feeling crept in: part of me started to feel like a retired player. I didn't have any events planned, and I wasn't sure when I would travel for competitions again. Chess had always been my world, and suddenly, that world felt paused.

Finally, in June 2021, the chance to return came. I flew from Chennai to Zagreb, arriving almost a month before the Croatia Grand Chess Tour Rapid & Blitz tournament. This early arrival was necessary because of COVID-19 safety rules that required quarantine before playing. Travelling during a pandemic was no longer simple. The usual rush to arrive just before a tournament had disappeared. Instead, there was waiting and planning like never before.

A few weeks before, in May, the Grand Chess Tour organizers invited me to participate in five major tournaments over the next three months. It was exciting news, but it also came with little notice. At that time, India was still facing a serious second wave of COVID-19 and many travel restrictions were in place. One tournament scheduled in Romania was cancelled. That was disappointing, but looking back, I realized it was probably for the best. I wasn't fully ready to compete at such short notice, and safety was the priority.

Settling into Zagreb was a relief. Thanks to the Indian ambassador and tournament organizers, I found a comfortable place to stay. The quarantine period gave me time to reflect, study chess and get ready mentally. After quarantine, I enjoyed walking through the city, meeting old friends and slowly feeling the familiar excitement of competition returning as other players arrived.

But just a week before the tournament started, something unexpected happened. I had a panic attack. It felt like my mind was overwhelmed with doubt and fear. Despite all my preparation, I wondered if I was truly ready. Playing chess online, coaching others and commentating during my break had kept me connected to the game, but nothing compares to the pressure and energy of playing live in front of a crowd. At the press conference before the tournament, I smiled and tried to show confidence, but inside I was questioning everything.

The tournament itself was tough. In the rapid rounds, I finished seventh – not exactly what I hoped for. But the blitz rounds were a different story. I found my rhythm and won two games against Garry Kasparov, one of the greatest players ever. Those wins felt like small victories that reminded me I still belonged. I finished second overall in the tournament. While not a championship, it was a positive step back into competitive chess.

This success helped me prepare for a special match against Vladimir Kramnik in Dortmund. What made this match unique was the rule that no castling was allowed. Castling is a special move in chess that protects the king by moving it behind a line of pawns and a rook. Without castling, the king is more vulnerable, which makes the game riskier and more creative. Dortmund is one of my favourite chess cities, filled with great memories. Winning this match was a proud moment – it showed that even after time away, I could adapt and compete creatively.

Though the basic rules are the same whether you play online or over the board, the experience is very different. In Zagreb, the hospitality, the face-to-face friendships and the energy of the live event made it special. Online chess, while popular and convenient, often lacks that personal touch. Behind a screen, it's easy to hide. And sadly, cheating has become a growing problem, especially among casual and younger players.

Some might think cheating is a new or clever trick. But fairness has always been a concern in chess. In big tournaments, strict security measures stop players from using hidden devices or getting outside help. Online, it's harder to catch cheaters because no one is physically watching. This temptation sometimes leads players to break the rules.

Chess websites now use powerful computer programs that can detect suspicious moves – those that don't match a player's usual skill level. But cheating isn't just about a few strange moves. It breaks a promise every player makes when sitting down to play: the promise of fair play. Chess is not just about winning or losing; it's about respect and trust.

I learnt this lesson deeply during an online charity event I played in 2020. It was a simul – where I played several opponents at once – to raise money for a good cause. One opponent, a young entrepreneur, played at a level far beyond what an amateur should be capable of. Later, he admitted to using a chess engine, a computer program that helps find the best moves. Unfortunately, others in the event did the same.

Cheating isn't just a mistake or pressing the wrong button. It's a conscious choice to cross a line. Using an engine means planning and following the computer's moves instead of your own. It's a serious breach of trust.

To fight cheating, chess needs more referees, stronger rules, and bigger consequences for those who cheat. Technology advances quickly, and the chess world must keep up. But the root problem goes beyond rules and technology. It comes down to what motivates us as people – our values, choices and how we treat others.

At its heart, chess is a game about honesty and respect, much like life itself. How we value fairness and integrity reveals who we are. It's a lesson I try to share with my family and students every day. And it's one I hope every player, young or old, will carry with them throughout their lives.

Playing chess isn't just about moving pieces on a board. It's about playing honestly, trusting your opponent and respecting yourself. Those lessons don't end when the game finishes. They stay with you, helping you grow – not just as a player but as a person too.

VISHY SAYS

WHETHER IN GAMES, SCHOOL OR LIFE, HONESTY AND FAIRNESS MATTER THE MOST. CHEATING MIGHT SEEM LIKE A SHORTCUT, BUT IT BREAKS TRUST – WITH OTHERS AND YOURSELF. TRUE SUCCESS COMES FROM FACING CHALLENGES HONESTLY, RESPECTING YOUR OPPONENTS AND PLAYING BY THE RULES. SOMETIMES THE HARDEST BATTLES ARE ABOUT STAYING TRUE TO YOUR VALUES, EVEN WHEN NO ONE IS WATCHING. THESE LESSONS HELP YOU GROW AS A PERSON, NOT JUST AS A PLAYER. WHATEVER YOU DO, REMEMBER THAT INTEGRITY IS THE STRONGEST MOVE YOU CAN MAKE.

44

LEARNING TO PLAY, LEARNING TO GROW

When I was younger, winning was everything to me. Success was like the engine that made everything move – without it, nothing mattered. I would get so excited by a victory and so upset by a loss that sometimes it felt like my whole world depended on the outcome of a single game. But as I've grown older and played more chess, my attitude has changed a lot. Now, when I win, the strongest feeling I have is gratitude – thankfulness for the chance to play, for the hard work paying off and for the support I've had along the way. And when I lose, I don't get stuck worrying or feeling bad for too long.

I've realized that worrying is like walking down a dark, blind alley – it doesn't help, and the only way out is to turn around and move on. I still want to win, but I'm no longer obsessed with big games and titles. It doesn't mean I've stopped trying to succeed; it just means that the trappings – the pressure, the stress, the fear of failure – don't control me anymore. It's almost like moving from being chained to winning, to being free to enjoy the journey.

Another thing I've learnt is to be kinder and more forgiving to myself. Failure doesn't have to be a bad word. Of course, if you lose all the time and never improve, that's a problem. But if you accept that losing is part of the game and use it as a chance to learn, it stops feeling hopeless. Over the years, I've had to change my goals and expectations. I can no longer pretend to be one of the very best players in the world all the time – I'm not, and that's okay. I think it's important to be honest with yourself about what you can do right now, and to set goals that make sense for where you are. Otherwise, you risk feeling desperate and frustrated.

Sometimes my results in tournaments are all over the place. I've had long stretches where nothing goes right – bad moves, bad luck, tough opponents – followed by surprising wins that come out of nowhere. This pattern can be hard to understand, but I've learnt not to focus too much on each individual game or tournament. Instead, I try to see the bigger picture – my overall progress, the lessons I'm learning, and how I'm growing as a player and a person. That perspective helps me stay steady, even when things aren't going well.

When I hit a long break from playing or a run of bad results, I don't get discouraged. I see it as a chance to learn something new. I look back at my recent games and study how other players have dealt with problems similar to mine. Sometimes that means learning from younger players, which is a great experience because they bring fresh ideas and new energy to the game. For example,

Levon Aronian has been a very tough opponent for me, and by trying to understand his style, I've picked up new ways of thinking about chess. The same goes for Magnus Carlsen and Fabiano Caruana – when someone beats you several times, it shows you that their way of understanding the game might be stronger in certain areas, and that pushes you to adapt and improve.

Chess is not just about knowing your own strengths but also about understanding your opponents'. If someone beats you a few times, it's important to respect their skill and figure out what they do better. That kind of challenge forces you to grow. It also means being curious and willing to explore new ideas, even if they don't feel natural at first. Sometimes I notice opponents doing well in openings or strategies that I haven't tried before, so I study those areas to add to my own game.

This constant learning, this curiosity, has been one of the most important parts of my career. It means always being open to change and ready to unlearn things that aren't working anymore. Unlearning can be hard because it means admitting that something you believed in might be wrong. But if you don't do it, you get stuck. Chess, like life, is always changing, and if you want to keep growing, you have to change with it.

There have been times when chess has been oh so frustrating. Sometimes the results go against you for a long time, or you face unfair situations, like when the chess world was split and there were fights about how the championship should be run. In those moments, I've thought about quitting – walking away from tournaments, the pressure, the whole game. But then

I remind myself that passion is what matters most. You don't have to be number one to find joy and meaning in what you do. What keeps me going is the love I have for playing chess – the warm, familiar feeling I get when I sit down at the board.

Now, my goals have changed. I'm not chasing rankings or titles as fiercely as before. I play for the joy of the game, to meet old friends and new challengers, to test myself and to savour the moments of victory, no matter how big or small. I think this is a stage every player goes through – moving from chasing success to finding freedom in the game itself.

Because the game is more than a game to me; it has been a game-changer for life.

VISHY SAYS

WINNING FEELS AMAZING, BUT LOSING IS OFTEN WHERE REAL LEARNING HAPPENS. WHEN YOU MESS UP OR FACE TOUGH PLAYERS, DON'T PANIC OR GIVE UP. INSTEAD, FIGURE OUT WHAT WENT WRONG AND TRY NEW STRATEGIES. SUCCESS ISN'T ABOUT NEVER FAILING – IT'S ABOUT GETTING SMARTER EACH TIME YOU PLAY. FOCUS ON IMPROVING YOUR GAME, NOT JUST THE SCOREBOARD. THE BEST PLAYERS KEEP ADAPTING AND STAY CURIOUS, EVEN WHEN IT'S HARD. THAT'S WHAT MAKES YOU STRONGER – NOT JUST A TROPHY WINNER.

45

BEING A PARENT (THE OTHER SIDE!)

Like many fathers and sons, my son Akhil and I share a strong bond. When I was younger, I often had different views from my own father. Now, when Akhil and I disagree, I sometimes smile and think, 'Ah, so this is how my father must have felt!' The shoe really is on the other foot now. And of course, parents today have to accept that we're no longer the 'experts' on everything – thanks to Google and AI!

When I chose chess as my career, it must have felt like a very unusual world to my father, who worked in a government job with the Railways. Akhil also enjoys chess, but he has found his own set of interests and has the confidence and courage to enjoy them without feeling pressure to follow his companions. I encourage him to follow his passion – because everyone needs to find their own path.

We enjoy travelling together, and we talk about movies, music and everyday things, and exchange songs of our times, just like any dad and son. I tell him stories about my struggles and experiences, and he shares what's happening in his life. It's not a one-way lecture; it's a two-way street.

VISHY SAYS

EVERY GENERATION MUST FIND ITS OWN PATH AND FOLLOW ITS OWN DREAMS, BUT LOVE AND RESPECT MAKE THE JOURNEY FUN TOGETHER.

46

MORE THAN A GAME

As I've grown older and experienced more of the chess world, I've realized that the game is about much more than just moves on a board or trophies on a shelf. Chess has taught me lessons that reach far beyond the 64 squares – lessons about life, patience, curiosity and courage.

One of the biggest lessons is about change and acceptance. When you play chess for many years, you learn that your strengths shift, your style evolves, and the game around you changes too. The players you faced 10 or 20 years ago are different people now, and so am I. In the early days, I dreamt of being the World Champion – and that dream came true. But time moves on, and the reality of ageing, new talents and changing priorities means that you have to adjust your goals.

It's natural to want to keep playing at the highest level forever, but I know I can't. The thought of still competing when I'm ranked far lower than my best makes me uneasy. I want to leave the game on my own terms, with my pride intact. That means paying attention to the signs that say it's time to stop competing seriously and start a new chapter in life.

What might that new chapter look like? For me, it means sharing what I've learnt with younger players – helping them find their own path, avoid mistakes I made, and understand the joys and challenges of chess. In India, chess is growing rapidly and remarkably. When I started, there were very few players who made chess their career. Now there are dozens of talented young Grandmasters with dreams as big as mine once were. It's exciting to see this new generation, and I want to be part of their journey.

Besides coaching and mentoring, I also want to keep playing chess in a more relaxed way – for fun and friendship. Chess tournaments are not just competitions; they are places where old friends meet, share stories and enjoy the game together. I think there's a special happiness in that, one that doesn't come from winning trophies but from being part of a community.

Chess has also taught me about patience and perseverance. The path to success is rarely a straight line. I've had stretches of amazing wins and stretches of disappointing losses. Sometimes it feels like no matter how hard you try, the results just don't come. But the key is to keep going, to keep learning and to never lose your curiosity.

I remember a funny story from early in my career. After becoming a Grandmaster, I was travelling by train to another event. Sitting next to me was a man who asked what I did for a living. When I said I was a chess player, he smiled and said, 'That's not a very secure job, unless you're Viswanathan Anand.' I didn't tell him I was Anand! But I liked that he thought of me that way – it made me feel proud and a little famous.

Chess has also brought me unexpected moments of joy and surprise. After winning my first World Championship title in 2000, when I returned to Chennai, I was greeted with cheers and applause from people I didn't even know. A public bus driver stopped his vehicle, got out and ran over just to shake my hand. Moments like that remind me that what we do can touch others in ways we don't always expect.

Sometimes I'm mistaken for a film actor or someone else famous, and I smile and thank the fans. These small moments show me that life is full of surprises and laughter, even in serious sports.

Chess is also connected to the bigger universe in unexpected ways. For example, there's a minor planet named after me – '4538 Vishyanand'. It's not a planet like Earth or Mars but a celestial object orbiting between Jupiter and Mars. I think it's amazing that my name is up there in space, and I often check its position online just for fun.

As I reflect on my career and life, I see that the game has been much more than winning titles or earning fame. It's been about the battles I fought, the friendships I made, the challenges I overcame and the joy I found in every move. Chess taught me to be patient, to be curious, to be courageous and to keep learning – lessons that I carry with me every day.

Now, when I look at my son Akhil, I see some of myself in him. Like me, he prefers puzzles and quiet challenges to the rough-and-tumble of football games or the endless jogging tennis requires. Instead, he enjoys solving problems, much like I did as a young boy with my chess books.

I want Akhil to understand that every medal or trophy has a story – a story of hard work, setbacks, perseverance and sometimes luck. More than that, I want him to see that success is not just about the prize but about the journey – the passion, the struggle and the joy of doing what you love.

Chess has been my passion since I was a child, and it still is. It has given me so much more than I ever expected. Even now, after many years and many achievements, I still find new challenges and new reasons to love the game.

Whether you're playing chess or pursuing any dream, the most important thing is to keep your passion alive. Success may not come quickly, and sometimes the world might doubt you, but if you keep learning, striving and believing in yourself, you'll find your way.

The voice of your dream – that quiet hope inside your head – is what will carry you through the toughest times. Keep it alive. Because that's how true champions are made – not just by winning but by loving what they do so much that winning becomes a bonus, not a burden.

VISHY SAYS

LIFE IS MORE THAN JUST CHASING TROPHIES OR REWARDS. AS YOU GROW, YOUR SKILLS AND GOALS WILL CHANGE – AND THAT'S PERFECTLY NATURAL. REAL SUCCESS ISN'T ONLY ABOUT BEING THE BEST, BUT ABOUT LEARNING, ADAPTING AND STAYING PASSIONATE, EVEN WHEN THINGS DON'T GO YOUR WAY. WINNING FEELS GREAT, BUT WHAT LASTS IS THE LOVE FOR WHAT YOU DO AND THE LESSONS YOU GATHER ALONG THE WAY.

JOIN ME IN A GAME!

Top Tips from Milestone Matches

47

MANUEL AARON V. VISWANATHAN ANAND (0–1)
(WHITE) (BLACK)

1982 DISTRICT TEAM CHAMPIONSHIP, MADRAS

BLACK WINS

At the Tal Chess Club in Chennai, started by Manuel Aaron, I spent hours playing, learning and asking endless questions.

In 1982, I won the Tamil Nadu State Junior Championship with a score of 6 out of 7. When I played against Manuel Aaron in this game, I wasn't yet dreaming of becoming a Grandmaster. I just wanted to play well and enjoy the game. Still, the win felt like a reward for everything I had learnt and practised up to that point.

I especially remember move 29: Nxd4. White had hidden its pieces cleverly – the king, queen and knights were all lined up on the kingside, and a rook was ready to attack. It looked hopeless. But then, Black brought in one more piece. Suddenly, it was like an army getting fresh reinforcements in the middle of battle. The side that seemed trapped suddenly had new hope.

VISHY SAYS

IN CHESS AND IN LIFE, NEVER GIVE UP TOO EARLY – SOMETIMES ONE SMART MOVE CAN CHANGE EVERYTHING!

48

VISWANATHAN ANAND V. JOEL BENJAMIN (1–0)
(WHITE) (BLACK)

1989 HOOGOVENS TOURNAMENT, WIJK AAN ZEE

WHITE WINS

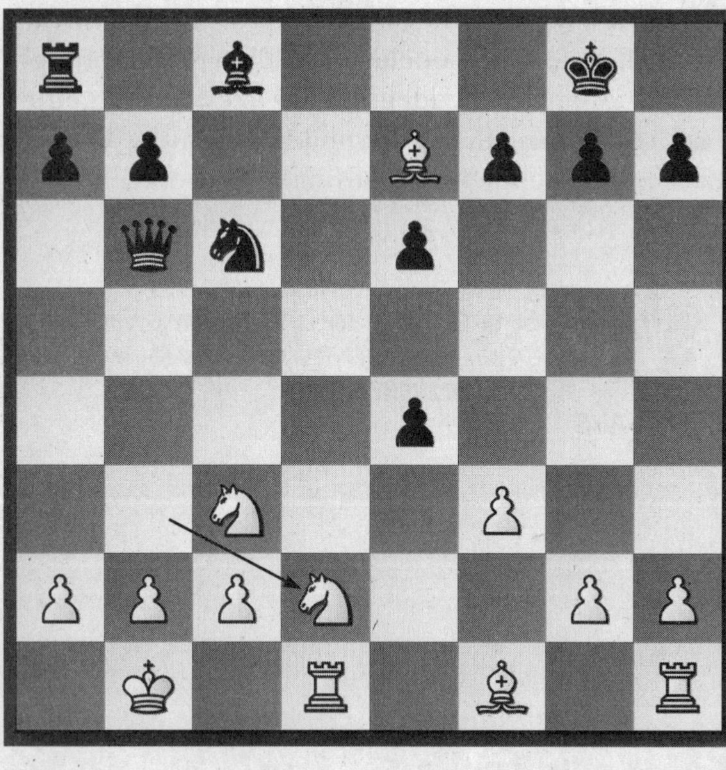

I made my debut at the 1989 Hoogovens Tournament in the Netherlands and completely amazed everyone by sharing first place with three top players – Predrag Nikolić, Zoltán Ribli and Gyula Sax – with a score of 7½ out of 13.

In round 12 of that tournament, I played against American Grandmaster Joel Benjamin and won the game in just 31 moves. That win helped secure my place at the top of the leaderboard.

At this point in the game, if Black recaptured my bishop after I'd played Nxd2, both my knights could attack Black's queen, and it would have to be given up. I hadn't prepared this line, but suddenly a conversation I had with Vassily Ivanchuk on the Catalan Opening popped up in my head, and I could sense a similar pattern here in the Sicilian Defence, even though the two are quite far apart. I went ahead and executed it.

VISHY SAYS

THINGS YOU LEARN OR TRY MAY SEEM SMALL NOW, BUT THEY CAN SURPRISE YOU BY HELPING IN BIG WAYS LATER.

49

VISWANATHAN ANAND V. ALEXANDER BELIAVSKY (1–0)
(WHITE) (BLACK)

1993 PCA QUALIFIERS, GRONINGEN

WHITE WINS

The PCA Qualifying Tournament was an 11-round event with 54 players. I was young and full of confidence, so I chose a sharp line against Beliavsky, even though he might have been well prepared. Luckily, it worked! I found a move that gave Black tough problems. Once I was in, there was no turning back – I just gave it everything. In the end, I tied for first place with Michael Adams, scoring 7½/11, and qualified for the Candidates.

VISHY SAYS

BIG RESULTS COME WHEN YOU PREPARE WELL, STAY BRAVE AND GIVE IT YOUR ALL.

50

ILYA SMIRIN V. VISWANATHAN ANAND (0–1)
(WHITE) (BLACK)

1994 INTEL CHESS GRAND PRIX, ACTIVE (BLITZ), NEW YORK

BLACK WINS

In 1994, I played a blitz Armageddon match in New York against Ilya Smirin. Armageddon means there can't be a tie – someone has to win. Since I had Black, I only needed a draw to go through, but I actually ended up winning.

Then came a strange moment. On just move 4, I suddenly froze. In blitz, you only have a few minutes for the whole game, so every second matters. But I sat there for 1 minute and 43 seconds – an unusually long pause in such a fast game! The usual move was right in front of me, but I felt there might be a hidden danger. My hand was ready to play, yet I held back, letting the clock tick while I waited for my mind to settle. That long pause gave me the clarity I needed. I figured out Smirin's plan, found my way through and, under huge time pressure, I not only survived but went on to win.

Looking back, taking the time to think calmly through my next moves, even while pressured for time, turned out to be a good decision.

VISHY SAYS

IT'S BETTER TO PAUSE AND THINK CLEARLY AT AN IMPORTANT MOMENT THAN TO PLAY WHILE YOUR MIND IS UPSET OR CONFUSED.

51

VISWANATHAN ANAND V. GARRY KASPAROV (1–0)
(WHITE) (BLACK)

GAME 9, 1995 PCA WORLD CHAMPIONSHIP, NEW YORK

WHITE WINS

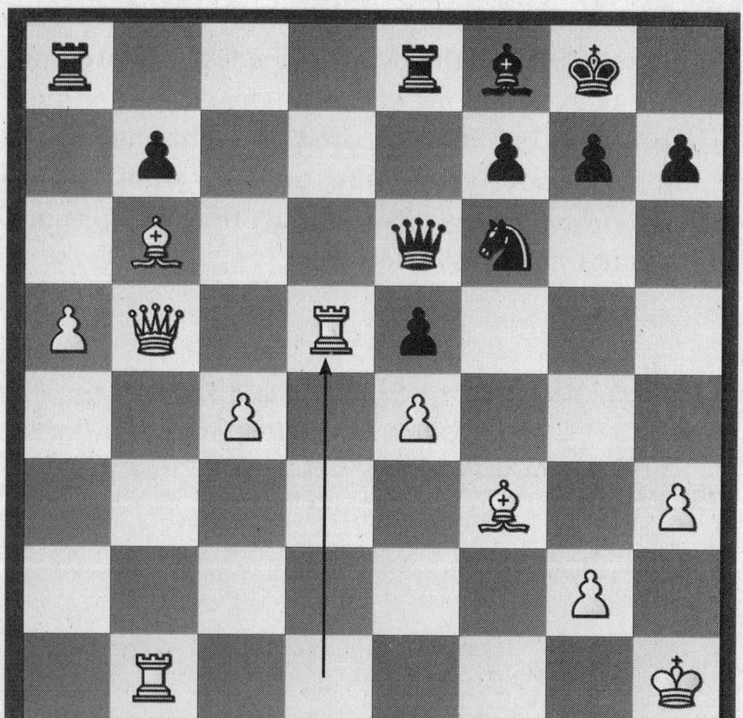

This match was played in an amazing setting – the 107th floor of the World Trade Center in New York City. The first eight games were all draws, a record for World Championship matches at the time. In one game, I played rook to d5. I was sure Kasparov wouldn't dare take it, because my pawns were strong. But he did! That gave me the chance to win my only game of the match in just 35 moves.

That match in 1995 changed me. Until then, I was happy to play good games and win sometimes. But after facing Kasparov, I knew I had to push harder if I really wanted to be World Champion. I realized that I needed to be flexible, unpredictable and strong under pressure. Most importantly, I had to truly *want* it.

VISHY SAYS

IF YOU REALLY, REALLY WANT SOMETHING, YOU HAVE TO WANT IT BADLY ENOUGH TO WORK ON IT. DOING BETTER THAN 'VERY WELL' NEEDS THE WILL TO GIVE IT EVERYTHING.

52

VISWANATHAN ANAND V. GATA KAMSKY (1–0)
(WHITE) (BLACK)

GAME 9, 1995 CANDIDATES TOURNAMENT, LAS PALMAS

WHITE WINS

In this tournament, Kamsky won the very first game – because I lost on time! But that was his only win. I struck back by winning Games 3, 9 and 11, all when I had the White pieces. By this stage, the match was tied.

All the years I had spent studying the Ruy Lopez opening (also called the Spanish Opening) finally paid off. On move 26, I played Nd1 – a creative move that blocked his knight and prepared to attack the weak pawn on b5. This game is one of the most imaginative I've ever played. In the end, I defeated Kamsky with a final score of 6½–4½, winning three games, drawing seven and losing just one.

VISHY SAYS

THE WAY I SEE IT, TALENT IS A LOT LIKE A PLANT. IT ONLY GROWS WHEN YOU WATER IT WITH HARD, SMART WORK. THAT MEANS NOT JUST TRYING BUT ALSO KNOWING WHAT YOU WANT AND USING YOUR SKILLS WISELY TO GET THERE.

53

VISWANATHAN ANAND V. VLADIMIR KRAMNIK (½–½)

(WHITE) (BLACK)

GAME 2, 2008 WORLD CHAMPIONSHIP, BONN

DRAW

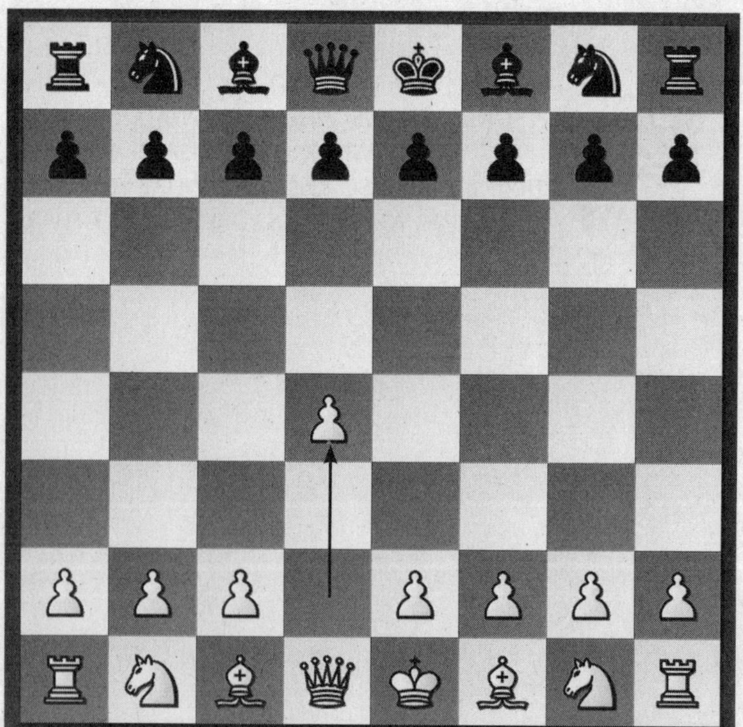

This match took place in Bonn, Germany, in October 2008. It was a 12-game World Championship match. I was the defending champion, and my challenger was Kramnik.

In Game 2, I had a big surprise ready. Instead of starting with 1.e4, which was my usual move, I played 1.d4. I had kept this plan secret for a long time. Of course, I was nervous – taking such a risk is never easy. But a year earlier, I had decided that I had to take bold steps, accept the results and prepare for them. My team and I worked hard, and now it was finally time to use that preparation. The plan worked, and after 11 games, I kept my world champion title with a final score of 6½–4½.

VISHY SAYS

IF YOU DO THE SAME THING EVERY TIME, PEOPLE CAN PREDICT YOU. SOMETIMES YOU NEED TO SURPRISE THEM WITH SOMETHING NEW. BUT MAKE SURE YOU PREPARE WELL AND TRUST YOURSELF WHEN YOU TAKE THAT LEAP.

54

VLADIMIR KRAMNIK V. VISWANATHAN ANAND (0–1)
(WHITE) (BLACK)

GAME 3, 2008 WORLD CHAMPIONSHIP, BONN

BLACK WINS

The 2008 World Championship match was set for 12 games. In Game 1, I played Black, but the game ended in a quiet draw. In Game 2, I surprised everyone by starting with 1.d4 instead of my usual 1.e4. It was a bold choice and gave me a small edge and some confidence, but that game too ended in a draw.

Then came Game 3. Here, my move Rg4 became the highlight of the game. Finding such a move is not easy – you can spot it but still hesitate, asking yourself, *'Is this really going to work?'* What made it special was that it allowed me to use months of hard preparation. Of course, you can never be fully prepared for everything on the board, and I still had to figure things out as the game unfolded. But having that preparation gave me a big head start.

I broke through. The win gave me the lead in the match. Still, I reminded myself not to celebrate too soon. Kramnik pushed back strongly, but with the clock ticking down, I kept control and converted the game into a clear win.

VISHY SAYS

I'D LEARNT THE HARD WAY THAT RELAXING TOO SOON CAN COST YOU THE GAME. A LEAD ISN'T THE SAME AS WINNING – YOU HAVE TO STAY CALM, FOCUSED AND GROUNDED. IF YOU START DREAMING OF VICTORY TOO EARLY, IT CAN SLIP AWAY.

55

VESELIN TOPALOV V. VISWANATHAN ANAND (0–1)
(WHITE) (BLACK)

GAME 12, 2010 WORLD CHAMPIONSHIP, SOFIA

BLACK WINS

This was the very last game of the championship. The score was tied at 5½–5½, which meant that everything depended on this one game. Whoever won would take the title, and if it was a draw, the match would go into tie-breaks. All through the match, I often felt like nothing was going the way I had planned. In game 11, I even came very close to losing, and the tension was at its peak. Then, in a sudden twist, my opponent made a mistake, and the balance shifted in my favour. It was like a door had finally opened after being shut for so long. The whole match had been full of emotions, surprises, and ups and downs. That's why, when I finally felt things turning my way in the last game, it was one of the most unforgettable moments of my career.

VISHY SAYS

RESILIENCE MEANS NOT GIVING UP WHEN THINGS GET TOUGH. HARD TIMES CAN COME SUDDENLY, LIKE A STORM. ACCEPT WHAT'S HAPPENING, BELIEVE YOU STILL HAVE A CHANCE AND USE YOUR INNER STRENGTHS TO GET THROUGH IT. IF YOU KEEP SAYING 'I CAN'T', YOU'LL OVERLOOK THE STRENGTHS YOU ALREADY HAVE.

56

LEVON ARONIAN V. VISWANATHAN ANAND (0–1)

(WHITE) (BLACK)

ROUND 4, 2013 TATA STEEL CHESS TOURNAMENT, WIJK AAN ZEE

BLACK WINS

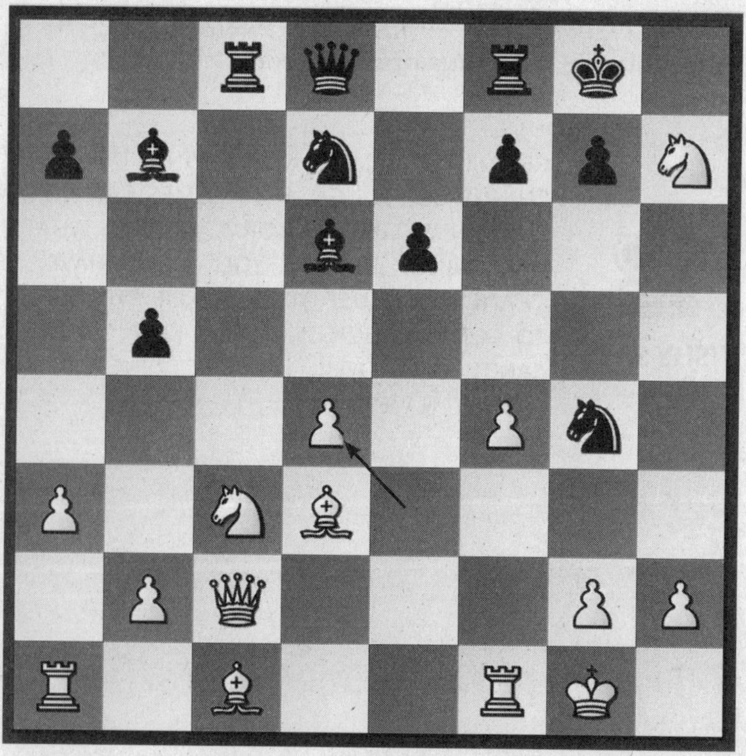

This memorable game with Levon Aronian took place in round 4 of the 2013 Tata Steel Chess Tournament in Wijk aan Zee. It became famous for a sparkling tactical sequence and fearless creativity, and people even began calling it 'Anand's Immortal'.

In chess, when people say, 'Someone's Immortal', they mean a game played by that person that is so brilliant and unique that it will be remembered forever, as part of chess history, almost as if the game itself is immortal.

This is probably the best game I've ever played because of how beautiful the ideas were. I wasn't fully ready for this line, and even though I remembered a little about it, many of the details were fuzzy. Since my team had studied it before, I decided to trust myself and spend time searching for the right move. Then a small but powerful thought struck me – the knight needed to land on the d3 square. I spent almost 30 minutes figuring out how to get it there. I knew that even if it left me with less time later, once I solved this puzzle, the rest of the moves would come together smoothly.

VISHY SAYS

LIFE IS ALWAYS CHANGING, SO IT HELPS TO STAY FLEXIBLE. WHAT WORKED BEFORE MAY NOT ALWAYS WORK AGAIN. IF YOU STAY OPEN TO NEW IDEAS AND ARE READY TO ADAPT, YOU CAN FACE CHALLENGES WITH CONFIDENCE AND FIND THE RIGHT WAY FORWARD.

57

VISWANATHAN ANAND V. BORIS GELFAND (1–0)
(WHITE) (BLACK)

GAME 8, 2012 WORLD CHAMPIONSHIP, MOSCOW

WHITE WINS

After I lost the seventh game, I stopped worrying about falling behind – because I *was* already behind. I even felt like my World Champion title was slipping away. So, I decided on a new approach: instead of stressing, I would just focus on making Gelfand fight hard in every game left.

Right away, this attitude paid off. In the next game, Gelfand made a mistake, and with my move Qf2, I took full advantage of it. I understood how he must have felt, but I was also hugely relieved. After his big win in Game 7, I struck back with an even bigger win in Game 8 – finishing in just 17 moves, the shortest winning game ever in World Chess Championship history.

VISHY SAYS

SUCCESS CAN TRICK YOU INTO THINKING YOU'RE UNBEATABLE AND DON'T NEED TO GET BETTER. BUT LIFE GIVES SMALL WARNINGS FOR A REASON. IF YOU NOTICE THEM, THEY CAN STOP YOU FROM GETTING LAZY AND SHOW YOU WHERE TO IMPROVE. EVEN WHEN YOU'RE FEELING LOW, THESE SIGNS CAN GUIDE YOU TO START AGAIN.

58

VISWANATHAN ANAND V. PETER LEKO (1–0)
(WHITE) (BLACK)

ROUND 2, 2017 WORLD RAPID CHAMPIONSHIP, RIYADH

WHITE WINS

In this game, I tried to build a calm, steady pressure and converted in the late middlegame/endgame – a win that helped launch my title-winning run in Riyadh.

At this point, I had an uplifting feeling – not the kind that has blood gushing through your veins, but a sense of satisfaction. I'd offered a piece, but Black didn't take it. Then I offered another, and he didn't take that either. Then I made a third knight move. The board looked beautiful here. I would rather score a point than play a beautiful game, but when you can do both, it becomes really special.

VISHY SAYS

IN LIFE, JUST LIKE IN CHESS, YOU SHOULD KEEP LEARNING – BOTH NEW THINGS AND NEW WAYS TO LEARN. SOMETIMES THIS MEANS 'UNLEARNING' OR LETTING GO OF IDEAS AND HABITS THAT NO LONGER WORK. TO MAKE REAL PROGRESS, YOU HAVE TO FIND THE REAL CAUSE OF THE PROBLEM – BECAUSE WHAT YOU THOUGHT YOU KNEW MIGHT NOT BE RIGHT.

PIECE BY PIECE

The Power of Every Move

59

KING: ∞ (INFINITE) POINTS

I AM THE KING, the most important piece on the board. I can move only one square at a time, but in every step, I carry the power of the queen, rook and bishop. I don't act much at the start, letting others take the lead, but every move I make is crucial. I must stay protected because if I fall, the game is over. I may be slow, but I am the heart of the board, guiding the battle. Even a single careful move can change the course of the game. My safety decides who wins and who loses.

VISHY SAYS

EVERY SMALL STEP COUNTS.

60

QUEEN: 9 POINTS

I AM THE QUEEN, the true powerhouse of the board! I can move across every square like the rook and glide along the diagonals like the bishop. I can strike in every direction – forward, backward, sideways or across – catching opponents by surprise. I can use both axes to stay safe while watching the whole board. I am fast, clever and unstoppable, able to protect key squares and challenge enemies all at once. With me on the board, anything can happen, and no one can match my power, reach or speed. I am the most feared piece in the game.

VISHY SAYS

COMBINE YOUR TALENTS TO SHINE.

61

ROOK: 5 POINTS

I AM A BIT OF A BOSS on the board! While the bishop and knight are limited to certain squares, I can move straight across the board, along rows and columns, as far as I want. I am strong and steady, able to control long paths and guard important squares. I am the king's loyal companion, ready to help him in every corner of the board. I can even join forces with another rook for castling, moving the king to safety while showing off my power. I am the ruler of straight lines, and my presence can shift the game in an instant.

VISHY SAYS

STRONG AND STEADY WINS THE DAY.

62

KNIGHT: 3 POINTS

I AM SPECIAL – the only piece that can jump in an L-shape, moving to squares that no other piece can reach. My jumps are powerful because I can leap over other pieces, going over anything that stands in my way. Every time I move, I change the colour of the square I land on, switching from light to dark and back again. I can make clever attacks that surprise the opponent and even catch their most important pieces off guard. I am full of tricks and surprises, and no other piece – not even the queen – can match my agility. I am truly one of a kind.

VISHY SAYS

BEING DIFFERENT CAN BE YOUR SUPERPOWER.

63

BISHOP: 3 POINTS

I AM THE BISHOP, master of my diagonal! I can only move along the squares of my colour, but within my path, I am unstoppable. I can zoom across the board in a single move, sliding past other pieces with silent speed. I will never meet the bishop on the other diagonal, but together we control almost every corner of the board. I strike from afar, surprising pieces that think they are safe. My long reach and sharp moves make me clever and powerful, and no one can match my sweeping influence that can change the game in a flash.

STICK TO YOUR PATH AND SHINE.

VISHY SAYS

64

PAWN: 1 POINT

I AM THE PAWN, the building block of the game. It's easy to underestimate me, but games have been won and lost because of how I am used and the walls I help create against opponents. I have a special, almost magical power – if I reach the other side of the board, I can transform into any piece I want! I also control key squares and can block or open paths for other pieces. A strong pawn structure can make it hard for the opponent to attack or create opportunities for a winning move. I may seem small, but I can change the game.

VISHY SAYS

SMALL STEPS CAN LEAD TO BIG CHANGES.

CLOSING GAMBIT

When I started playing chess, even books about the game weren't easy to find, and there was hardly a chess community like there is today. News about games reached us one or two months later! The very first chess book I found was an *Encyclopaedia of Chess* by an American writer, and to me it felt like the Final Truth. That world has transformed. Now, information is available in seconds. Search engines have replaced encyclopaedias, and databases have replaced libraries.

A long time ago, chess games could go on for seven or eight hours! Players used old ticking clocks, and a common rule was 2½ hours for the first 40 moves, then an hour for the next 20. If the game was still not finished late at night, it was stopped. The player whose turn it was had to secretly write their next move on a slip of paper, seal it in an envelope and hand it to the referee. The next day, the envelope was opened, the move was played on the board, and the game continued. This was called an adjournment.

In the 1990s, everything began to change. Digital clocks came in, which allowed players to get a few extra seconds per move – this is called an increment. Games now had to be finished the same day, so adjournments disappeared. A typical new rule was two hours for the first 40 moves, then an hour for the rest of the game, plus 30 seconds added per move. Today, most classical games are even shorter, usually 90 minutes for the whole game, with 30 seconds added per move.

And then came the faster formats. Rapid chess gives each player 25 minutes, plus 10 seconds added per move. That means a whole game can be finished in about 50–60 minutes. Blitz is even faster – three to five minutes per player, sometimes with just two seconds added per move. A blitz game can be over in the time it takes to eat a snack! And then there's bullet, the fastest of all, with only one minute per player. Bullet is played mostly online and is hugely popular around the world. Chess has moved from very long games with sealed envelopes to faster, fairer contests that are always completed in one sitting.

As computers grew stronger, new rules were needed to make sure play stayed fair. At big events, players now pass through metal detectors to check that they aren't carrying electronic devices. Phones, smartwatches and even outside pens are not allowed. Games shown online are often delayed by 15 minutes so that no one can secretly use a computer to give advice. And since chess is recognized as a sport by the International Olympic Committee, there is also drug testing at world championships and Olympiads to make sure no one uses substances to improve focus or reduce stress.

The way chess is broadcast has changed too. In the 1990s, people followed games in newspapers or magazines. Today, every big game is shown live on the internet with computer analysis, expert commentary and instant replays. Millions of fans from anywhere in the world can watch. Players too have changed their methods – earlier they studied from books and practised on wooden boards; now they train with databases, chess engines and online platforms. This means openings are deeper and preparation is sharper than ever. The average age of top players has dropped, because youngsters learn quickly with modern tools.

Tournament formats have also become more exciting. Knockouts grew popular in the late 1990s, leading to today's World Cup, where classical, rapid and blitz games are all mixed. Official rapid and blitz world championships were introduced in the 2000s. New formats and faster styles have brought new energy.

These changes over the decades have also brought new countries into the spotlight. India, for one, has seen a huge rise in chess players. Today there are many Indian players to cheer for on the world stage, and the chess community here is one of the most vibrant anywhere.

So much has changed – the clocks, the formats, the technology, the way people train and watch. But one thing has not changed: the nature of competition. You still need preparation, analysis and the right moves. Chess has only grown stronger from these changes, with live broadcasts, instant sharing and powerful learning tools. It has never been easier to enjoy the game or work at it.

If you aren't a chess player already, now's the time to set up the board, make your move and join India's chess story.

Hope you liked reading about mine!

ACKNOWLEDGEMENTS

Gratitude seems like a small word to describe what I feel towards most people mentioned here.

My parents, without whom I would never have been able to give myself to chess so freely. My father, for always telling me to be myself and play fast if that's what felt good. My mother, for waiting patiently for my phone call after every tournament just to hear my voice.

My siblings, for putting up with the fact that I was always the pampered and preferred one, and for supporting my chess.

Aruna, for being my punching bag par excellence and for holding me up in my darkest moments.

Akhil, for showing me every day that fatherhood is by far the most exhilarating experience I will ever have.

Hans-Walter Schmitt, for sharing my taste in music, especially Queen, but more than that for being the one person I know who would take a bullet for me.

Maurice and Nieves, for being my 'other' parents – their love and laughter will always stay with me.

My seconds, for working tirelessly by my side and for dealing with my chess and me. They taught me to learn, unlearn and, for the most part, tolerated my music and my long walks.

Rajendra Pawar, Raji, with whom my association goes beyond the NIIT connect, for making me feel like a part of his family and celebrating my victories in the most spectacular fashion. In many moments, we took inspiration from each other's journey.

The Westbridge Anand Chess Academy, which we started with Sandeep Singhal and his team at Westbridge. It has been so amazing to see young talent and travel with them as they experience their chess journeys. It has been most exciting to also learn about giving advice while having received it all through my career.

My fans, for always being kind to me and for their constant encouragement that has kept me going through tough challenges.

For Susan Ninan and Poulomi Chatterjee, a special thank you, for their untiring work in collecting and collating material for the book and doing an excellent job of telling my story in my words. The many hours they spent with me helped me relive pleasurable memories.

IBD
25600
12/01/26